THE 3 HEAVENS

A STUDY IN SPIRITUAL WARFARE

MARK GORMAN

Mark Gorman
2000 Mallory Lane Suite 130-347
Franklin, TN 37067 USA
(866) 663-2043
www.markgorman.com

ISBN-10 0-9761428-2-1
ISBN-13 978-0-9761428-2-9

Design: DREAMBOXCREATIVE.COM

CONTENTS

FOR WE DO NOT WRESTLE AGAINST FLESH AND BLOOD, BUT AGAINST PRINCIPALITIES, AGAINST POWERS, AGAINST THE RULERS OF THE DARKNESS OF THIS AGE, AGAINST SPIRITUAL HOSTS OF WICKEDNESS IN THE HEAVENLY PLACES.

❧ EPHESIANS 6:12 (NEW KING JAMES VERSION)

CHAPTER 1

THE THREE KINGS

We are all aware that the Bible was not originally written in English. Often, in studying the Bible, we must go back to the original text in order to get a better understanding of what was actually being said. A case in point is found in the words of Jesus in Matthew 28:18 KJV: "All power is given unto Me in heaven and in earth..."

Jesus does not have all power in heaven and earth. This is not a trick statement - it is a fact (I like getting you frustrated with me right up front).

You may ask how I know that Jesus does not have all power in heaven and earth. First, I know that satan has power. If you don't believe that, just take a look around you at all the lives being devastated by satan's power.

I've heard preachers say that satan can't touch a child of God. In fact, growing up in church, I heard a few sermons in which they told us: "...When your big brother Jesus died on the cross of Calvary, He pulled all the devil's teeth. And now, all the devil can do is roar. He is just a roaring lion."

First of all, I cannot find any scripture in the Bible which says that Jesus performed oral surgery on the devil. Secondly, if satan is seeking whom he may devour, what does he need in order to devour us? Unless he plans to "gum us to death", he must still have his teeth.

It is dangerous to take your theology from tradition, rather than truth. We'll talk more about that later, but for now, I wanted to at least state the fact that, if you can't find it in the Bible, don't build a doctrine around some man's opinion.

It concerns me when I encounter Christians who spend most of their time shouting, "I've got the devil under my feet. I've got the devil under my feet." My word of caution is: "Just make sure that Jesus is in your shoes." If you have the devil under your feet, and carnality and flesh in your shoes, you will be snake-bit.

A few years ago I received a phone call from a pastor. I was scheduled to speak in his church for the first time that following month. He said, "Mark, I understand that you are a teacher. Could you tell me what subject you teach on?" I informed him that I teach on several different topics, but that my favorite one is probably spiritual warfare. He said, "That's what I was afraid of." He then informed me that he did not believe in spiritual warfare, and declared: "We believe that when Jesus died on Calvary, He defeated satan. Now he cannot touch a child of God. All we have to do 'til Jesus comes, is to fight the good fight of faith." (Of course, I immediately wondered who they were fighting in the good fight of faith, since satan had apparently "left the building".)

First of all, Jesus did defeat satan. That's a given! But let me ask you something. A few years ago, Evander Holeyfield defeated Mike

Tyson in a championship boxing match. (I understand it left a bad taste in Tyson's mouth.) If you have ever seen Mike Tyson in the ring, you know that he is a formidable opponent. My question to you is: "How would you like to fight Mike Tyson?" Obviously he can't hurt you because he was defeated. Do you see how silly that argument is? We need to understand the difference between the words defeated and destroyed.

When Jesus died on Calvary, satan was defeated, but he wasn't destroyed. He is still around.

If satan can't touch a child of God, then why did God tell us to wear all this armor? Do you wear shoulder pads to watch a football game? Do you wear a catcher's mask to watch baseball? If we are only sitting in the stands shouting, "Get 'em, Jesus! Get 'em, Jesus!", then why do we need armor? The way I figure it is, if satan couldn't touch us, Jesus would have just said, "Dress casual".

(If you can survive my sense of humor, I really think you will get something good out of this book).

It is obvious to me that if Jesus told us to put on armor, we need to get ready to fight. Satan was defeated, but he isn't destroyed. In the next few chapters as we look deeper into the subject of spiritual warfare, we will see that everything we struggle against in the physical realm has roots in the spiritual realm. Whether you choose to fight or not, warfare is happening right now. It is time to put on armor and fight back.

If Jesus doesn't have all power in heaven and earth, what was He saying? The Greek word used in that verse is *exousia*, which means authority. Jesus said, "All authority is given to Me in heaven and in earth." Satan has power, but he does not have God's authority. Jesus has it all!

In Matthew, chapter 8, we read the story of a man who came to Jesus on behalf of his servant who was ill. In verse 9, he said, "...I am a man under authority, having soldiers under me: and I say to this man, Go, and he goeth; and to another, Come, and he cometh; and to my servant, Do this, and he doeth it." Why did he say that people did what he told them to do? Was it because he had authority? No. It was because he was under authority.

The first principle we must understand about authority is that it is not a commodity which we possess. We don't have authority. Satan doesn't have authority. Jesus has it all.

Rather than a commodity, authority is a flow. All authority flows out from Jesus, since He has it all. When we are under authority, it flows through us, much like water flows through a pipe. We become the conduit for the flow of God's authority.

One of my favorite verses is James 4:7: "Submit yourselves therefore to God. Resist the devil, and he will flee from you." But let us be honest. Have you had times when you tried to resist the devil and he did not flee? I have! Does that mean that this verse doesn't work? No! It only means that we are not "doing" the whole verse.

Before God told us to resist, He told us to submit. The word submit means to "place under". When we submit ourselves to God, we are placing ourselves under God - under His authority. When we are under that flow, the authority flows through us. As we resist the devil, he flees - not from us, but from the authority which is flowing through us. Now, think back to all of those times when you tried, unsuccessfully, to resist the devil. In every case, you have to admit that you were not submitted to God.

Who was James addressing when he told them to submit themselves to God - Christians or sinners? Obviously, he was writing to Christians. If he told Christians to submit themselves to God, it becomes apparent that a person can be saved and not submitted.

Growing up in church, I had the concept that if you were saved, you were automatically submitted - and if you were not submitted, you were not saved. We lived under a constant fear of losing our salvation. (Buckle your seatbelts! If you grew up in the type of church I did, you may experience some mild turbulence in the next few paragraphs).

People have asked me if I believe a person can lose their salvation. My answer is, "If by lose, you mean misplace, 'No.' I don't believe you can misplace your salvation." I know I am being facetious, but with good cause. I grew up thinking that I could lose my salvation without even realizing it had happened, much as you would lose a set of keys. Today I don't believe that is possible.

In the story of the prodigal, Jesus does not speak of the "prodigal backslider", "prodigal heathen", or "prodigal reprobate". He speaks of the prodigal son. Think about it! What was he when he left home and broke his father's heart? He was a son. When he was living it up in the world and enjoying the party scene, what was he then? A son. When he had lost everything, had no friends in sight, and was eating with the pigs, what was he? He was still a son. When he came to his senses and made his way back home to his father, what was he then? He proved that he was a true son. Amen

This shakes up my theology, too, but it is a story Jesus told, and I am sure He told it correctly. The bottom line is this: real sons come home. He did not enjoy the privileges of sonship while living in rebellion. In my opinion, if he did not return home, he would have forfeited his rights as a son.

Do I believe that a person can lose their salvation? No, but you can walk away from it and never look back. Believe me, if you give up your salvation, it will be with full knowledge on your part.

You can be saved, and not submitted. Don't assume that just because you are a Christian, everything is O.K. Many people believe that because they have a relationship with Christ, they have access to His authority. That is a foolish presumption on their part.

July 1, 12

IN CHRIST We Become (the Kingdom)
Not Just in it But To Become it.

Take a look at the seven sons of Sceva. Do you remember the story in Acts, chapter 19? They tried to cast out demons in the name of Jesus. Many Christians say that if you're a child of God, all you need to do is speak the name of Jesus and demons will flee. Take a look at what happened in this story. The demons said, "We know Jesus, but who are you?" They then caused the demonized man to attack the seven sons of Sceva, sending the sons of Sceva away, naked and wounded.

People have told me that this was because the seven sons of Sce-va were not saved. Get real! When is the last time you saw a sinner trying to cast out a demon? They were saved, but not submitted.

Remember this principle in spiritual warfare: your authority in using any spiritual weapon is determined by your submission to that weapon. The reason some people are more effective in using the Name of Jesus is because they are more submitted to Him.

Jesus was speaking to Christians in Matthew chapter six when He told them to "seek the kingdom of God." You may ask, "Didn't He just mean to seek heaven?" No. Although heaven is part of the kingdom of God, it is definitely not all of the kingdom of God. To understand the kingdom of God, you must first understand what a kingdom is. A kingdom is any place where the king's authority is obeyed without question and without hesitation.

Simply stated, this means that in a kingdom, only one person votes. Who votes in a kingdom? The king! If you want to know who the king is in any kingdom, find out who has been voting.

Heaven is part of the kingdom of God, because in heaven, God's authority is obeyed without question and without hesitation. In heaven, God has the only vote.

On one occasion, Jesus was teaching, when some people asked Him, "When will the kingdom of God come?" They were looking for a physical kingdom with palaces, thrones and crowns. Jesus said,

"Don't you know that the kingdom of God is in you?" If I am to seek God's kingdom, I don't need a telescope to try to find God's kingdom. I need a mirror.

If you were to ask the average Christian, "Is God the King of all of your life?", they would probably say, "Let's use the process of elimination. Is satan king of any part of my life? No. Therefore, God must be King of all my life." They just missed an entire king. There are not just two kings in this world - God and satan. There is a third king, and his name is "self". How do I know that self is a king? Because he votes - and in a kingdom, only kings vote. When does self vote? Only...on a constant basis. Only when he's awake. Why does self vote so much? Because...of all the opinions I've ever heard, mine is my favorite. Don't you feel that way? That's why we love to vote.

For those of you into philosophy, let me give you something to ponder, "I vote ... therefore, I am." (that'll keep 'em busy for a while).

You may be asking, "How does self vote?" Well, let's take a look at a hypothetical situation. How does God vote on forgiveness? He's for it. He voted in favor of forgiveness. So you come to Him and say, "You know, Lord, I know that in most situations, it would be a pretty much cut and dried matter, that I should just forgive and move on. But I feel that there are certain extenuating circumstances in my particular situation which would give merit to further investigation into the possibility of justifying a prolonged period of bitterness before we actually begin the forgiveness process."

Now, I'm willing to admit that you presented a pretty good argument but you still voted. If God says forgive, and you don't... you voted. Congratulations! You're the new king. Doesn't that feel great?

Yes, it feels wonderful to be king until you realize that, in every kingdom, the king is responsible for two things: protection and provision. If God is the King, He protects and He provides. If you're the king, get busy!

Let's say that a guy gets saved and filled with the Holy Spirit. His wife and kids are serving the Lord with him. They're involved in Church. But one Sunday the pastor preaches on tithing. All the way home from church, this guy "manifests". He says, "That preacher had better mind his own business. That's my money. I earned that money. It's mine. I'll say how much money I'll give to the church. That preacher had better leave my money alone."

Do you know what that sounds like to me? A king! He's voting. He's in charge of his finances.

> *For those of you who have read my previous book, "God's Plan For Prosperity", some of the principles you are about to read, may seem somewhat redundant. To others, it may seem that I am repeating myself. HA! To both groups I would say: This is with good reason. Actually, this book, "The 3 Heavens", was written long before "God's Plan For Prosperity". When we were preparing to publish "The 3 Heavens", God spoke to me in a time of prayer, and instructed me to put this book on "pause", and write the book on prosperity first, and to publish it before this book. I don't fully understand His reasoning, but I trust Him enough to obey. It would have been impossible to properly address the topic of "tithing" without including some of the principles you are about to read in this chapter. The good news is that, after this chapter, there shouldn't be much else in this book which repeats what you read in my first book, "God's Plan For Prosperity".*

I can just hear someone saying, "But isn't it true that tithing is not taught in the New Testament?"

My answer:… "No, not if you remove 3 books – two of the gospels and the book of Hebrews. But what's 3 books among friends? Just rip those 3 books out of your Bible, and then you can say that tithing isn't mentioned at all in the New Testament. After all, you'd still have 63 books left, plus the concordance, and maps."

Do you see how ridiculous that is? If tithing is mentioned in

3 books in the New Testament, then it is mentioned in the New Testament.

I never cease to be amazed at the people who try to reason their way out of tithing, not realizing that they're voting. If you're not familiar with the principle of tithing, the Bible teaches us that the first 10% of everything that comes into our hands belongs to God.

You know, I can handle it if the reason they wanted to argue tithing is so they could have the right to give 15%. I mean, if just one person walked up to me and said, "Tithing's not taught in the New Testament. I'm giving 20% and you can't stop me." I'd say, "Go for it." But typically, the person who wants to argue tithing is trying to see how little they can do and still get by. What a beautiful concept!

Wouldn't you love to have this guy working for you? "I know you said that I have to be at work by 9:00 o'clock every morning, but I was wondering, how late I could come in, on a consistent basis, and not lose my job." "I know you said that I only have 10 sick days a year, but I was wondering, like, how much work could I actually miss and still get paid." "I know you said that I had to do this much productivity to meet my quota, but I was wondering how little could I actually do and still get paid, and not lose my job."

Wouldn't you love to have this guy working for you? Yet we come to God with the same attitude, and say, "Look, God, I can't do this 10% thing, but I'll tell ya what I'm gonna do. I'll go half. I'll go 5%. O.K.... 6%. O.K.... split the difference, 7.5%. Its my top offer." And we think God should be giggling all over 'cause we offered him 7.5%.

Let me 'splain you somethin'. If you give 9.9%, you voted. Because God voted for 10%.

You may ask, "Well, Mark, isn't it true that tithing was just in the Old Testament?" No, tithing is taught not only in the gospels, but in the book of Hebrews.

Some say, "Tithing was under the law." No, tithing started with Abraham, over 500 years before the law. How can you say that tithing was under the law, if it was 500 years before the law?

You may say, "What if you're wrong, Mark?" (Which I'm not!!) "What if tithing was under the law only, and now we're under grace?" Well, you should be doing twice as much under grace, as you were doing under the law, so you should be givng 20%. My suggestion is that you should stick with the 10% and be grateful.

You may say, "I know why you're talking about tithing. If you ever speak at my church, you want me to put my tithes in your love offering." No. The tithe belongs in the church. It does not belong to some guest speaker or to some television evangelist, or to your cousin, who lost his job. It belongs in the church, period. It's the next 20% that goes to the guest speaker. (Do you see me smiling? That was just a joke. There isn't a verse that says that you should give the guest speaker 20%.)

After speaking at a conference in Florida, a lady came up to me and said, "Young man, how dare you tell me that I cannot give my tithe to the poor!" I said, "Ma'am, you can give 90% of your income to the poor, but don't mess with God's 10%."

Let's get back to the guy who refuses to tithe. Let's say he hears about spiritual warfare and decides he wants to get involved in the work of God. He says, "Binding and loosing - nice concept. I like it. Why don't we do this. Next Tuesday night, we'll have some people over for coffee, then we'll do a little binding and loosing, and get into the whole warfare scene."

So Tuesday comes, they have their coffee, and then they decide to do some warfare. They say, "Name a demon, and we'll bind him. Just name that demon!" What they don't understand is, that warfare means "You shoot and they'll shoot back." If you shoot and they don't shoot back, that's called murder. But since God called us to warfare, we know that they will shoot back. That's why we must be wearing the whole armor of God.

I'm amazed at the Christians who think that they have on the armor of God just because they're saved. Remember, He didn't say, "Congratulations, you're now wearing the whole armor of God!" He said to put it on. That means that you can be saved, and be missing His armor.

You may say, "Well, I don't have to worry about that because every morning when I wake up I say, 'I put on the helmet of salvation; I put on the breastplate of righteousness; I have my loins girded about with truth; I have my feet shod with the preparation of the gospel of peace; I have the sword of the spirit in one hand and the shield of faith in the other. I'm ready!'" Not if you're voting!

Think about it, how do you put on the whole armor of God? By submitting. When God is the King of my thought-life - when He has the vote on every thought, my mind is submitted to Him, His authority flows through my mind and forms a helmet of salvation around it.

It's difficult to submit every thought to God. Do you ever have these people come up to you and say, "Oh, I never have a problem with my thought-life", as they look down their noses at the rest of us? I always feel like saying, "Well, you have to have a thought-life first!"

When God is the King of my emotions, my attitudes and my relationships, they are submitted to Him, and His authority flows through my emotions, forming a breastplate of righteousness around me.

Although the Bible only tells us of six specific pieces of armor, I personally believe that there are as many pieces of armor as there are areas in our lives in which we can vote. We put on armor by submitting and we remove armor by voting.

"Well, if that's true, then what am I putting on every morning when I go through the whole routine of naming each piece of the armor of God?" That's called the "emperor's new clothes".

Here, we have this guy doing warfare, who refuses to tithe. He's voting in his finances. So where do you think he's missing armor? In his wallet!

Satan attacks him in his finances, and he comes home from work and says, "Honey, this is just an attack of the devil. It is the spirit of poverty. I'm just going to fast and pray for the next three days, and believe God for a miracle in our finances."

He may as well eat! No amount of fasting and prayer will make up for his rebellion against God's authority. It is an insult to God's inteligence for me to willfully vote, in rebellion against His authority, and then ask Him to protect, and provide for my kingdom.

A few years ago I received a phone call from a man in another state. He had gotten our number from his pastor. He explained that, when I was in his church, I had prophesied over him - that God had shown me thngs about his childhood and his past and that he now owned his own business. He said that I prophesied that financial blessings would come into his life in ways that he had never dreamed of. I asked what had happened. He said, "It was amazing! Money started coming in from everywhere! It was more money than I had ever seen." I said, "Well, what happened?" He said, "It stopped. In fact, now, I'm worse off than I was before. I owe everyone."

I began praying for him, binding the spirit of poverty and the spirit of debt - loosing back into his life, everything that satan had stolen from him. In the middle of my prayer, God stopped me and said, "You don't have authority to pray that." I said, "But, Lord, I give 20% of my income! What do you mean, by saying that I don't have authority?"

God said, "It's not your money you are praying about, it's his money. Ask him if he tithes."

I stopped in the middle of my prayer and said, "Brother, do you tithe?......Brother, are you there?" From the other end of the phone, a frail voice said, "Do you mean, like, now?" I said, "Like, yes." He said, "Well, I'm not tithing now. I can't afford to. I owe too much money."

I said, "Well, then, I can't pray." He said, "What do yo mean, you can't pray? You prophesied over me. I called you and asked you to pray. Why can't you pray?"

I said, "Because, you don't have authority to pray. God isn't the king of your finances, you are." He said, "But I told you I can't afford to tithe." "Let me tell you somethin'," I replied, "You have one creditor who is bigger than all the rest. If I were you, I'd pay Him first." I'd much rather owe a credit card company money than to owe God.

I believe that there are three basic reasons why Christians tithe faithfully and still have financial difficulty.

The first reason, I believe, is "testing". This is the answer we've heard all our lives. Every time we'd ask someone why we weren't prospering, they'd always say, "It's a test." My question was, "When is this class over?" When I was in school, we took a test, we passed or failed, but then we moved on. It sounded to me like we are supposed to be going through perpetual testing.

I do believe that, on occasion, God will allow us to see our true motives, by temporarily withholding the blessing. He doesn't want us to come to church thinking it's time to barter.

Too often, we find ourselves with the attitude of almost bringing a calculator to church to compute what God owes us. "Let's see, I gave $127.39."

As a side note, I am always amazed by these people who won't round up their tithe check to the next dollar, like its going to break the bank for them to give God that extra 61 cents. I know there's no verse that says "Thou shalt round up", but it just sort of bugs me. Let me just suggest something to you; just one time, swing on out there and give God that extra 61 cents, and feel like a big boy! As I said, there's no scripture on this, it's just one of my little pet peeves.

But anyway, you have this guy with his calculator saying, "I gave $127.39. So let's see, You owe me..." Do you want God to tell you what you own Him? I believe that, on occasion, God allows us to see our true motives. Will we be faithful, and give out of relationship, or are we only giving for what's in it for us?

The second reason why Christians tithe and still have financial difficulty is poor stewardship. I have Christians come to me and say, "I thought God was going to supply all of my needs. But I can't pay my bills."

My response, "God didn't fill out all those credit card applications." Some people walk into a store and say, "Pick a card, any card." You know they're in trouble when they say, "Can I pay my Visa with my Mastercard?"

Let me just tell you something. If you are living your life on credit cards, life is 18% - 22% more expensive for you than for everyone else.

You may be wondering why I know so much about credit cards. Let's not get into that. Because of the nature of my traveling ministry, paying for hotels, airfares, rental cars, etc., it would be unwise for me to carry that kind of cash. Gina and I still use credit cards, but we make a commitment to pay them off at the end of each month.

I recently read an article in a major newspaper which said that the average American owes $2,500 on their credit cards. Now I realize that there are those who have gone above and beyond the call of duty, and they are above average, owing well over $2,500. But let's just talk about the average folks.

This article stated that if you paid 18% interest on the credit card and paid the minimum each month, it would take 30 years to pay it off, and in the process you would pay over $11,000 in interest plus the $2500 principal. There is no way that can be considered as good stewardship.

I believe that God loves us enough to withhold additional finances from being placed into wasteful hands. We know that He wants us to be blessed. God's word says, in Proverbs 13:22, "A good man leaves an inheritance to his children's children, But the wealth of the sinner is stored up for the righteous." (NKJV) It is obvious that the inheritance spoken of is financial, since the remainder of the verse is also about money.

I know how much my wife and children can spend. To leave an inheritance, so abundant, that after my wife and children have been taken care of, there would still be enough for my grandchildren to fight over, that would be a lot of money! (I spoke with one man who said, "I don't even have life insurance, because when I die, I want it to be a real tragedy!")

Did you realize that most Christians could not afford to be a Good Samaritan? Think about what the Good Samaritan did. Could you, without a credit card, take a person who has been wounded and robbed, pay for their medical needs, drive him to a hotel, pay for a week in advance - cash, a week of breakfasts, a week of lunches, a week of dinners, and then turn to the man behind the registration desk and say, "I'll be back in a week. If he's charged anything else to the room, I'll pay that, too."

Can you imagine that? Could you do that - without credit cards?

It is my contention that God wants us to prosper to the extent that we are always in a position to reach out a helping hand, without taking food out of the mouths of our children. I don't know about you, but my definition of prosperity is two things: to be free from debt; and to have enough in my hand that I can bless someone else. I don't feel truly prosperous unless I am able to be generous with others. If you want to be like God, a giver. He loved us so much, that He gave the best He had. God is not a taker - He's a giver. He doesn't give what's convenient - He gives His best.

2 Corinthians 9:11 says, "You will be made rich in every way so that you can be generous on every occasion..." (NIV)

This passage makes two things very clear: First, God wants His people to be blessed with finances. Secondly, His purpose is, not only that we would be blessed, but also for us to be generous on every occasion.

Now, let's get back to the question of stewardship. I believe that when we exhibit good financial management, God will entrust us with more.

Remember the story of the talents, in Matthew 25. In verse 23, the ruler told the wise servant that because he had been faithful over a few things, he would now be made ruler over many.

The third reason why Christians tithe faithfully and still have financial difficulty is that they are not using the authority that is available to them. A few years ago, I was flying from New Orleans to Birmingham, Alabama, to preach at a church there. My first flight was from New Orleans to Nashville.

While sitting on the plane, God spoke to me and said, "Mark, you have been tithing faithfully for years. You have placed your finances under My authority and My authority has been flowing through that area of your life all this time. The problem is that you have not been using the authority that is flowing through you. I did not say that if you submit yourself to Me, the devil would flee. My word says that after submitting, you must resist him before he will flee. Use the authority that is in your hands, and resist the devil off of your finances. Command him to repay what he has stolen from you, and loose it into your hands."

Right there on the plane, I began praying, "Satan, I'm submitted to God in my finances. I can resist you and you have to flee. In Jesus' name, I take authority over you. Take your hands off of my finances, and loose into my life everything you have stolen from me, and pay it back seven times." (Proverbs 6:31 says that a thief must repay seven times what he stole.)

When I changed planes in Nashville, as I was waiting for my next flight. There was an announcement over the sound system, "Ladies and gentlemen, this flight has been overbooked. We need volunteers who will take another flight. If you will do so, we will give you a $200 travel voucher with our airline." I said, "That's me!" I got my ticket changed, and they handed me my $200 travel voucher.

Now, I had been re-routed to Atlanta, Georgia. On the plane, I said, "Well, it worked last time. -- Satan, I'm submitted to God in my finances. I can resist you and you have to flee. In Jesus' name, I take authority over you. Take your hands off of my finances, and loose into my life everything you have stolen from me, and pay it back seven times."

True story - when I got to the airport in Atlanta, they announced on the sound system, "Ladies and gentlemen, this flight has been overbooked. We need volunteers who will take another flight. We will give you a check, which you can cash immediately, if you will take another flight." Again, I said, "That's me!"

I called the pastor that I was to be with in Birmingham the next morning. I don't remember my exact words, but it was something like, "Pastor, exactly what time does service start tomorrow morning? We're gonna milk this thing for all it's worth!"

I finally got into Birmingham at 1:30 AM. I preached Sunday morning and evening.

On Monday, I had an early flight home. I was running a bit tight on time (those of you who know me are not surprised by that statement), and got to the airport just a few minutes before the flight. I asked if I could still make the flight. He said, "Oh, I don't know if you can get on the plane."

Then he yelled to his buddy and said, "Harry, can we fit anyone else on that plane?" Harry said, "Absolutely not! We're taking people off the plane right now!"

I interjected, "Would you like for me to take another flight?" He said, "Oh, sir, that would be so kind of you. Harry, don't worry, this nice gentleman said that he would be willing..." I interrupted, "Wait! Wait! Wait!... What'll you give me?"

By the time I got home, I had more money from the airlines than I received from that church - Thank God!

God taught me something. Authority does you no good unless you use it. Maybe you are doing much the same as I did. For years, I tithed faithfully, wondering when, and if, I might be blessed. I kept saying, "If I'll just be faithful, eventually, God will bless me." But that's not what the Bible says.

James 4:7 is quite clear. It does not say that if we submit ourselves to God, the devil will eventually leave. It says he will only flee if we resist him, using the authority we gain by submitting ourselves to God.

Now, I realize that I've spent quite a bit of time talking about money. In actuality, these principles apply to every aspect of our lives. You could use the very same strategy in any area of your life: thoughts, attitudes, desires, habits, relationships, past failures, past hurts, career goals, family, etc.

The reason I used money as an example is because it holds your attention! Also, I'm tired of seeing God's people oppressed in their finances. I want you to be blessed, as you use these principles in warfare for your finances - and for every area of your life.

"*Mark, God Bless you, Gina and your family. It is in great part because of you speaking at business conferences and your audios that my husband and I have come to Christ. We have humbly asked Him to forgive our sins and have made Christ our Lord and Savior. We would not have had the spiritual growth we have had without you. I don't believe without Mark that we would have ever read the Bible or become Christians.*"

A. I. FROM CALIFORNIA

CHAPTER 2

STRONGHOLDS

I AM A STRONGHOLD
OF CHRIST 2012
Sept 25

Growing up in a classical Pentecostal background, my concept of a stronghold was something "out there". When thinking of strongholds, I thought of bars, houses of prostitution, organized crime, and all of the evils of the world. Basically, to find a stronghold, I thought I needed binoculars. It never occurred to me that I might need a mirror to find one.

Stronghold is a military term. It speaks of fortified places of resistance. My definition for a stronghold is "a portion of territory that refuses to submit to the authority that is over the rest of the territory." When a general speaks to his captains about military strategy, he points on a map to show them all of the conquered areas. He will then point out the pockets of rebellion, which refuse to surrender. These are the strongholds.

A good example of a stronghold is the revolt staged by the brave students at Tianamen Square in Beijing, China in 1989. Tianamen Square became a portion of China that refused to submit to the

Communist authority which ruled over the rest of China. When the Communist government discovered the stronghold, they did the wisest thing they could do in terms of survival. They immediately squashed the rebellion and pulled down the stronghold. Personally, it saddened me to see them blow out this flame of hope for democracy in China, but I wish that we, as Christians, would learn from that incident and destroy strongholds in our own lives as soon as they are identified.

2 Corinthians 10:3 (KJV) For though we walk in the flesh, we do not war after the flesh: 4 (For the weapons of our warfare are not carnal, but mighty through God to the pulling down of strong holds;) 5 Casting down imaginations, and every high thing that exalteth itself against the knowledge of God, and bringing into captivity every thought to the obedience of Christ; 6 And having in a readiness to revenge all disobedience, when your obedience is fulfilled.

Look at the areas Paul tells us to deal with in order to pull down strongholds. 2 Corinthians 10:5 specifically addresses imaginations, knowledge and thoughts. These are all found in the mind. He tells us that in order to pull down the strongholds, we must conquer these mental processes. Think about it - whose mind can I change? The obvious answer is, "my own." That is the end of the list. You can't change anyone's mind, only yours.

Since Paul was writing to Christians, it becomes obvious that he was speaking of strongholds that exist in the minds of Christians. The strongholds are in our minds. They are in us! I had never seen it this way until God showed me, a few years ago, the strongholds in my own life.

What are strongholds? They are areas of rebellion in the life of a Christian -- rebellion against God's authority. It stands to reason that strongholds exist in the Christian and not the sinner. A strong-

I can Become A Stronghold For n wiel CHrist Against devil

hold only exists where the majority of "territory" is subdued.

It is impossible for a sinner to have a stronghold. If an entire country rebels against you, it is not typically called a stronghold. It is referred to as an "enemy nation". Therefore, the sinner cannot have a stronghold since none of his life is submitted to God. The only people who have strongholds are Christians, because we are the only ones in whom there is at least a part of our "territory" submitted to God.

Can you think of areas in your life where "self" is king where your thoughts, imaginations, or knowledge are not submitted to God? Do you struggle with the knowledge that, although you love God and want to serve Him, you recognize places in your life where you have rebelled against His authority?

The stronghold did not start out that way. It started as a thought. Of the three: imagination, knowledge and thoughts; the weakest are thoughts. A thought is so slight, we often underestimate its potential. In fact, a thought starts out so defenseless that Paul says we can "bring it into captivity". Think about it! When a thought enters your mind, it is very easy to dismiss. The thought is so weak that it seems to pose no threat. What we do not realize is that a thought is only the first stage in the development of a stronghold.

Basically, when a thought comes into our mind, we either accept it or reject it. Often, we "play" with a thought in the way we would play with a puppy or kitten, thinking it cannot harm us. We easily accept thoughts, which, in reality, could eventually threaten our spiritual man.

Remember that the thought is so small and weak, that if we simply choose to do so, we can bring it into captivity. We possess the ability to set up a tollbooth in our mind, which will enable us to check every thought before it comes in, to see if it is in obedience to

Bishop eHG All your THougHTS Are NoT your own.

Christ. If it is not, we can catch that tiny thought in our hand, as you would catch a gnat, and squash it.

An imagination, however, must be cast down. When a thought stays in our mind long enough, it begins to germinate. It is fed by our ability to fantasize or imagine. This is the growth stage of the stronghold. The thought in our minds then enlarges and expands so much that it takes up more and more of the space (territory) which once belonged to God's Kingdom. Sometimes, the imagination looms so large that we stand on our tiptoes, stretching to reach it, drag it down and conquer it.

If the thought has now grown into an imagination and remains unchecked, it becomes knowledge. At this point, it has become one more layer of bricks in the stronghold of your mind.

There are three basic areas in which we as Christians have strongholds. These are the same three areas in which Jesus was tempted in the desert: pride, fear and lust. Let us look specifically at each of these.

First, we will deal with lust. In today's terminology, lust speaks only of sexual desires. In reality, however, lust is any desire, which is out of control - not submitted to God. We can have a lust for alcohol, cigarettes, drugs, power, fame, sex, food, or anything that is out of the will of God. By itself, a lustful thought will never become an action. In order for a person to commit the sinful act in response to lust, there must also be pride.

Pride empowers us to rebel against God's authority. Without pride, lust merely produces a temptation to sin, which has not yet become an action. This is referred to as a latent desire. Many people have a yearning to commit certain types of sin. They may harbor these desires for years without giving in to them. Why don't they commit the sin? Because they fear the consequences.

It is only when pride rises within us that we feel immune to the consequences of sin and act out what we thought would always be only a desire. Many Christians are fooling themselves. They say, "It is alright for me to think about it and want it because I know I'll never do it. I'm too afraid to actually commit the act of sin." What they don't realize is that imagination fuels the passion of desire and eventually invites pride to be its partner in crime. This results in an act of sin, which we will later regret.

When my son, Kenneth, was seven years old, one summer he took a two-week trip with me. It was just the two "men". Male bonding! At that age, I didn't know how much he had listened to what I had been saying in the services. As we were driving back home to New Orleans, he began to ask me some thought-provoking questions. His first query took me by surprise.

"Dad, how can a spiritual being be seen in the physical realm?" I still don't know how I bluffed my way through that one.

He then asked, "Dad, what is lust?"

First, to help him understand the principles of God's kingdom, I asked, "Kenneth, do you know what a kingdom is?"

"Yes, sir," he replied, "a kingdom is any place where the king's authority is obeyed without question and without hesitation."

WOW! I knew he had been listening. We then discussed what that meant. Afterwards, I explained to him that lust is any desire that does not please God. I don't know if this was a perfectly accurate description, but it was the best I could think of to explain lust to a seven-year-old.

I further explained to him that lust does not become an action until pride is involved. I said, "Kenneth, you know that there are wrongful things you sometimes want to do. Although you desire to do them, you won't, because you fear the punishment for disobedience. But sometimes, if you think about it long enough, pride causes you to rebel, and you disobey anyway. That is when lust becomes an action."

When I was growing up, I heard many people preach on sinful actions. It seemed that sin was thought of only as an action and not as a thought. The focus was on the act, not on the thought. To me, that is like trying to keep a volcano from erupting by holding your hand over the top of it. If you don't deal with the fire inside, you will never stop the eruption.

The thought of lust may initially seem to be weak. In fact, you may be playing the game with thoughts of lust, thinking that they will never become actions. Don't be fooled.

Can you believe we have spent all this time talking about lust, and I still have two more points to cover? Let's move on...)

Fear brings paralysis. It is the opposite of faith. In fact, fear is the enemy of faith. An interesting thing to note is this:

Faith is believing that what I cannot see - will happen.

Fear is believing that what I cannot see - will happen.

Fear is faith in the negative. You are absolutely certain that something will go wrong. My contention is that if you have the ability to have fear; it stands to reason that you can have faith. You need only change your expectations.

The reason I say fear brings paralysis is because it removes our will to fight. Many Christians develop what I call "victim mentality". They believe that they need to "cope" with what is coming upon them. I can't find the word "cope" in the Bible. Instead, I find that God called us to "conquer". Don't cope with your circumstances - conquer them. Don't forgive your faults -- fight them! Don't wail with your weaknesses - war against them! Don't cope......conquer!

When I was in school I was always the smallest kid in the class. When I started attending junior high school, I finally met a guy who was smaller than me. I held onto him like you would hold a trophy. He was proof positive that I was taller than someone my age.

Being so small, I was constantly being picked on by the bullies in the class. The fear of what they might do kept me from retaliating. I tried to cope with everything they threw my way. Fear took away my fight.

Occasionally, however, they did something which made me so angry that my fear was temporarily forgotten -- I just had to get even! The Bible says, "Be ye angry, and sin not". (Ephesians 4:26) How is it possible to be angry without committing a sin? When you recognize that satan is the author of your frustration, you will do what I did in school. The anger becomes greater than the fear and acts as a natural defense mechanism. You forget the fear and attack your enemy.

Why do so many Christians live under the weight of fear? It is because they think they are the cause of their own problems. In our society we think of fear as a thought process. Yet, in 2 Timothy 1:7, we are told that fear is a spirit. If I think of fear only as a thought, I think of myself as the enemy, because I am the one who continues to dwell on the thought of fear. Picturing myself as the enemy causes me to bring condemnation on myself, which further perpetuates the problem.

However, when I understand that fear is a spirit, a demon, I can then direct my anger toward the demon, instead of being angry with myself. When you become angry at the demon of fear, you can do warfare against him.

Many Christians who do not understand this principle have allowed themselves to be intimidated and oppressed by fear. They have come to the place that they no longer try to defend themselves. They are just trying to "hang on". This is the "victim mentality" I spoke of earlier. They are trying to cope instead of conquer.

Often, a person's life will begin to manifest the very thing they fear. If they fear sickness, instead of fighting sickness, they just accept it; content to simply endure. I have seen people accept sickness after sickness, merely because they were afraid to fight back.

Recently, a godly woman asked me if I thought that maybe God wanted her to accept her sickness, rather than believe for her healing. I told her the only time that Jesus prayed "If it be Thy will" was when He was praying about God's direction for His life. It was not in regard to healing. As far as I am concerned, I will operate under the assumption that it is God's will to heal every disease and meet every need. If it is not His will, He can let me know. Until then, I will keep asking and believing.

It is difficult to distinguish between fear and caution. Oftentimes, in our attempt to be cautious and prudent, we give way to fear. We must ask God to give us the wisdom to distinguish between the two.

The third type of stronghold is pride. I consider this stronghold to be the most dangerous of the three. The reason is because it is hard to identify. First of all, with every stronghold of pride, you get a free set of binoculars. The first thing the pride demon tells you is, "You don't have any strongholds, but look at the strongholds in that person over there."

If you are reading this book, and you think that you have never had a stronghold, now you know what yours is! (I hope you will keep reading. If you stop here, who is telling you to quit?)

The stronghold of pride is very common in long-established churches, denominations, and organizations. It is a pharisaical spirit, which causes us to be judgmental and critical of others, while justifying our own actions and attitudes.

When computers were first developed, who would have thought that there would be such a thing as a computer virus? Today, entire corporations exist for the purpose of identifying computer viruses, developing programs to destroy them, and protecting computers against them.

The most dangerous type of computer virus is the stealth virus. Where have we heard this word stealth? That's right! The United States is very proud of our stealth bomber, an airplane which is considered to be one our most formidable weapons, because it cannot be seen on radar.

The stealth virus operates in much the same way. It is designed to hide itself in the computer so that it is undetectable, even to many of the sophisticated computer virus-protection programs.

Your most dangerous enemy is the one you cannot see!

Pride manifests itself in many ways. Not only does pride cause arrogance and egotism, it also causes rebellion against authority, and unforgiveness toward others. You may ask, "How is pride associated with unforgiveness?" If we didn't think we were worth so much, we wouldn't think we had a right to hold a grudge.

Be on a constant lookout for pride. It can manifest itself in something as subtle as a lack of gratitude for someone's gesture of kindness. Remember, without pride a lustful thought would not become an action.

Often people ask me if a Christian can have more than one stronghold. My reply is, "You are a child of God. You can have anything you want." (Once again, I hope you can appreciate my brand of humor.)

It started as a thought, but it ended as a brick wall of a stronghold. How could that little thought bring such devastation? It couldn't, if we didn't feed it.

When I was a teenager, I was convinced that thoughts were about the neatest thing in the world. I could think anything I wanted and nobody knew. I sat at the dinner table with my father, an ordained minister, my mother, a great woman of prayer, my brother and my sister. Here I was, sitting innocently at the same table, thinking my "terrible teenage thoughts". If Mother and Dad had known what I was thinking, they would have spit their food clear across the table. We're talking projectile vomiting!

I really thought I was "cool" - that I was getting away with something. What I didn't realize was that those teenage thoughts would grow into teenage imaginations, and the teenage imaginations would become teenage knowledge, and the teenage knowledge would build strongholds that would haunt me in my adult life.

You see, even in our childhood, satan begins laying the groundwork to build strongholds in our mind. Even though we may grow up in the best Christian home, our thought-life is our own. We alone have the vote in our thought-life. I believe that all Christians have had strongholds at some point in their Christian walk. If left unchecked, those strongholds will eventually dominate us.

You may ask yourself, "What is the danger of a stronghold anyway?" Remember, in every kingdom the king is responsible for two things: protection and provision. Who is the king of our strongholds? Obviously, it is self. How do we know this? Because self voted, and only kings vote. Therefore, if self is king, who is responsible to protect and provide for the stronghold? Obviously, self is.

Many people think that because they are saved, they automatically have the whole armor of God. As we discussed previously, you do not receive the armor of God at salvation. Paul told us to "put it on", which means we may be missing certain pieces of armor. Remember whose armor we are speaking of. It's the armor of God! Armor is used to protect. Whose kingdom does God protect? His own.

When we establish self as a king in a stronghold, we have relinquished our right to the armor of God in that part of our life. It doesn't mean that we have lost our salvation. It means that we lost our protection. When we establish a stronghold, we have peeled off God's armor in that area. We still have armor there, but it is supplied by the new king. We have the armor of self.

Of the three kings: God, satan, and self, which is the weakest? The answer is self. If self is not weaker than satan, then why was it necessary for Jesus to die on the cross? We could have defeated him ourselves. Jesus' death on the cross is conclusive evidence that self is weaker than satan is.

Because self is weaker than satan, our armor is no challenge to his assaults on our lives. We are basically defenseless. The armor of self is like a paper seat belt. It gives you a false sense of security. You sense there's something there, but it will be of no use in the time of danger.

Let us tackle a really controversial subject: Christians and demons.

When I was growing up in church, we were taught that a Christian could not have a demon. We didn't mention the words Christian and demon in the same sentence.....Not even the same paragraph. I figured you had to have been backslid for at least a month before a demon could come near you.

In fact, when we were talking about a sinner, we stated that they had a "demon", but a Christian had a "spirit". In talking about a sinner, we said, "Oh, he is a heathen..... he has a demon of alcohol as big as a bus." When speaking of a Christian, we commented, "Oh, she's a little widow woman.....has a little spirit of fear." In a sinner, it was a demon....in a Christian, it was a spirit. What was the difference? The closest I can figure is that the original Greek for spirit must be a demon with a coat and tie.

An interesting observation is that many Christians don't want you to say that a demon is at work in a Christian. Instead, they want you to say it is satan. Many Christians are more comfortable with the word "satan" than they are with the word "demon". But stop and think about it! Satan is the head of all demons. We just have this hang-up with the word "demon".

Some of you are asking that big question, "Mark, do you believe the demon is in you or on you?" My answer is, "Yes.......it really is!"

"Well" you say, "which one is it......in you or on you?" My response is, "What is the difference? Whether the demon is in you, on you, next to you, beside you, or behind you; he is too close!" Don't get caught up in semantics.

Let us get down to the real issue. Allow me to tell you why I changed some of my views on this. A few years ago, in the mid 80's, some of my heroes in the ministry started falling, and I needed answers. I was desperate for answers; so much so that I no longer cared about having my loins girt about with "tradition". I wanted truth.

I needed to understand how a person could be so mightily used of God in one area of his life, and so tormented by satan in another. I needed to know this, not only to understand these fallen leaders, but also to better understand myself.

For the record, I don't believe a Christian can be demon-possessed. My understanding of possession is basically ownership, or something close to it. I do believe, however, that a Christian can be demonized, that they can have demonic activity in their life. How is this possible?

It is very simple. Because a stronghold is the kingdom of self, and because satan is stronger than self, he has access to our strongholds. Don't try to blame everything on the devil. If we had not voted, if every thought had been brought into captivity, if imaginations had been cast down, he would not have had access. We opened the door.

If you are still having difficulty with the concept of demons, let me pour a little gasoline on the fire. When Peter tried to tell Jesus not to go to the cross, Jesus looked at Peter and said, "Get thee behind Me, satan." Understand what happened. Jesus looked at a Christian and talked to the devil. How could this be possible? I don't know if the demon was in him, on him, next to him, beside him, or just over his left shoulder, but he was close enough that Jesus could look at Peter and talk to the demon.

Some people think that Peter must not have been a Christian at the time. If that were true, then we would have a whole new set of problems. Just four verses earlier, in Matthew 16:19, Jesus gave Peter the "keys to the kingdom". Do you honestly believe Jesus would have given such awesome authority to a sinner? If not, then Peter was a Christian when Jesus looked at him and talked to the devil.

People have told me that they didn't believe certain preachers were saved, because of some of the things they saw later in their lives. In fact, they questioned whether those men had ever been saved. Get real! Look at how God used them! The real question is, "How could a man be so blessed in one area of his life and so weak in another?" This is the answer: one part of his life was submitted to the kingdom of God. God protected and provided for His kingdom, and it was blessed. The other part of his life was submitted to the kingdom of self. It was protected and provided for by self, so satan had access to that stronghold.

God showed me the mistake made by those fallen leaders and by myself. It is a misjudgment that you may have made also. When we are blessed in one area of our life, we often assume that means we have God's approval on all areas of our life. We must learn to distinguish between God's kingdom and the kingdom of self in our lives.

Don't assume that because God is blessing your finances, answering your prayers for the sick to be healed, and using you in the gifts of the Spirit that satan does not have access to other areas of your life. Although I do not believe that a Christian can be demon possessed, I am convinced that a Christian can have demonic activity in the strongholds they have established in their thought-life.

If you were buying a home and the seller said, "You won't ever have to worry about termites in this house. We have never had a problem with termites. It would be a waste of money to have a termite inspection. Don't even think about termites. You will never see a termite in this house." Would you have a termite inspection before you bought the house of your dreams? Of course you would!

The thing that amazes me is that for years Christians have listened to those who have said, "Christians can't have demons. A demon can't get anywhere near a Christian. Don't even look for demons." And what was our response? Most of us said, "OK, I won't even look for them."

Let me ask you, "Does it do any damage to a home when you do a termite inspection? If the termite inspection concludes that you do not have termites, are you disappointed? Do you feel that it was a waste of your time and money to have the inspection done?" Then ask yourself this question: "If they are right, and if Christians can't have demons anywhere near them, does it hurt to look?"

CHAPTER 3

How Strongholds Grow

There is a growth process - a natural progression that occurs in the development of a stronghold.

Let's say you have a fearful thought. The thought may be, "What if I have a disease?" "What if this elevator stops between floors?" "What if my family leaves me?" "What if this plane crashes?"

There are two options: You can either reject the thought or accept it. To reject it, you simply bring it into captivity. Then kick it out using the tollbooth in your mind to identify it and reject it.

What if, instead of rejecting the thought, you accept it? You tell yourself, "I'm just being careful - being cautious." In reality, however, you are opening the door for an enemy to infiltrate your mind.

It enters as a small item; a tiny, seemingly insignificant thought among so many thoughts in your mind. Scientists tell us that by the time we reach the age of thirty, our subconscious mind has recorded over three trillion memories. Everything I have ever heard, seen, smelled, tasted, or felt has been recorded in my subconscious.

How could this one little thought make a difference among three trillion others? Well...just give it some time.

Before you know it, you have started imagining the fear. The human mind is an amazing mechanism. The power of imagination is greater than most of us realize. While two people sit side by side, riding a bus home from work, the imagination in each mind allows one of them to ski the snow-covered slopes of New Zealand's Southern Alps. The person in the next seat sees himself dying from a fatal bus accident, although it never happens. They will both arrive safely home that day, one refreshed by the thoughts of a vacation holiday; and the other somber, but secure in the knowledge that he was "wise enough" to anticipate danger - just in case it ever happened. *Would've Could've - Should've*

Suppose Thinking As you imagine the potential outcome of your anxiety, the fearful thought swells with a growth that is being fueled by your own mind. You are feeding the thought with your imagination. Before you know it, you are envisioning what it would be like to die of a dreaded illness, to be stranded in an elevator between floors, to be alone after losing the family you love, or to experience those final seconds of terror as a plane crashes to the ground, in flames. In actuality, the chance of any of these things ever happening is extremely slight; but just in case, you have been wise enough to prematurely experience the misery anyway. Don't you feel ridiculous?

The next stage in the development of the "fear stronghold" is the final stage - knowledge. Now you know you have a disease. You haven't been to a doctor, but you have all the symptoms listed in your "Handbook of Diseases". In fact, you don't need a doctor. You can diagnose this yourself. You tell your family, "Stay away from me. I know I have something. It might be contagious. I'll quarantine myself. The only thing I can eat from now on is pizza or flounder, because these are the only things that will fit under the door."

Perhaps you have now come to the conclusion that since the elevator is traveling so slowly, you know it's going to stop any moment, and you will be trapped with all of these strange-looking people surrounding you on this ride. You are hyperventilating and breaking out in a sweat because you are positive that something will go wrong. You have faith that it will. Remember, fear is faith that something will go wrong.

You just know this plane is going to crash! You think, "That sound isn't normal. The pilot just gave an announcement a few minutes ago, and his voice sounded a bit shaky. Could it be that he already knew there was something wrong with the plane? Perhaps I am the wisest person on this plane because I am perceiving and anticipating the danger before anyone else. I need to warn them!" Suddenly you scream at the top of your lungs, "This plane's going down, man! Everybody put your head between your knees. We're about to crash!"

It started with a thought, then it grew into imagination, and it ended in knowledge.

What should you do with a thought of lust? It's just a little thought. And lustful thoughts are always so cute. It won't hurt. I'll just let it linger for a while.

Before you realize it, you are imagining: "What would it be like?...Oh, yeah, and what would that be like?...and some of that, too?" The imagination is becoming so powerful; it is under its own control, like a runaway train. Before long, you are saying, "I know I want some of that....and that, too.... and some of that over there!" THOUGHT - IMAGINATION - KNOWLEDGE.

Sometimes people say, "I can't help it! When that thought comes into my mind, it just snow balls. Before I know it, it becomes an action. I feel so helpless when it happens!"

By the way, we have a special project coming up for our ministry, and we need to raise money to pay for it. If you are reading this book, you should donate $10,000.00 per family member to that project. That means that if you have a family of five, you are expected to donate $50,000.00 to the project.

Did you see how quickly you threw that thought out of your mind? You are not still sitting there trying to figure out ways to come up with $50,000.00. (Well, actually, I hope some of you are.) You have just proven that if you don't want a thought occupying your mind, you will get rid of it. So, don't tell me that you couldn't stop that thought. Admit that you liked it. The reason we allow thoughts to stay in our mind is very simple. We like them, and we welcome them. I hate admitting that as much as you do. Nevertheless, only the truth will make us free.

Have you ever heard people relating how they "fell into sin"? Let's get a mental picture of that happening to you. You "fell in". How did you fall in? Did somebody leave the lid open? Please don't say that you "fell" into sin. If you sinned, you walked in!

As much as it pains me to say this, I must admit that every time I have sinned, I walked in with both eyes open, knowing it was sin. If you admit any less, you are lying to yourself. When we accept responsibility for our actions, it helps us to take charge of them in the future.

Your life today is a product of two things: the circumstances you have encountered and the choices you have made. So many people say that their lives are the result of their circumstances alone. There is no such thing as a circumstance without a choice. You always have a choice and the original Greek for "always" is "always"! You always have a choice. Don't state that you didn't have a choice. Remember the original Greek for "always".

Some of the most difficult thoughts to deal with are lust thoughts. One reason is that many of our lustful desires are actually natural desires, which have gotten out of control. The desire for food is a natural desire, but when it is out of control, it becomes gluttony. Gluttony is a form of lust. The desire for sex is natural. God created sex for us to enjoy within the confines of marriage. When this desire is taken outside of the marriage bed, it becomes lust. The challenge before us is to maintain the healthy, natural desires while keeping them in check - not allowing them to stray beyond the parameters of God's Will.

While I was ministering in a church several years ago, a young man came up to me during the altar service. I could see the worry and agony on his face. He said, "Brother Mark, I have this problem with lust. Every time I look at a woman, my mind begins to race with all of these lustful thoughts. I want you to pray for me that I will never want to look at a woman again." I said, "Not only will I not pray that, but if anyone ever does, and if it works, let me know. We ain't doin' lunch!"

You see, it is appropriate and proper for a man to find a woman attractive. It is only when that attraction to the wrong person grows into desire and passion that it becomes sin. If a man doesn't find women attractive, something is wrong with him.

I often find that we have little tolerance for the strongholds in our Christian brothers and sisters. A person with a fear stronghold looks at a person with a lust stronghold and says, "I can't believe he did that. His wife told him that if he got drunk one more time, she would leave him and take the kids with her. He did it anyway. Obviously, he doesn't love his wife or the kids." No, that is not true. What is obvious is that if you think like that, you don't have a clue! When he got drunk, he wasn't thinking of his wife, his kids, his reputation, his career, or his status in the community. He was thinking of one thing...the alcohol - his stronghold.

We interrupted the person with the fear stronghold while he

was still criticizing the man with the lust stronghold. How rude, to interrupt someone mid-criticism.

They say, "I would never do anything like that!" We know you wouldn't. You're too afraid. You are the one with the fear stronghold!

By the way, those of us who grew up in church may recall that it was assumed for years that sin was, by definition, an "action" - something we did. Because of this, the only stronghold that was significantly addressed in our lives was the lust stronghold. Lust is the easiest stronghold to recognize because it manifests in an action.

Fear, on the other hand, often goes unnoticed in the Christian life. Credit this, in part, to the fact that so many ministers used fear to keep us from giving in to lust. They did not realize that one stronghold was being exchanged for another. If the only reason you serve Jesus is a fear of hell, I have to keep reminding you how hot hell is, every time you come to church. What a pitiful existence! We should refrain from sin because we love Jesus - not because we fear hell. We want to please Him.

Another struggle with fear comes from our attempt to assimilate what the Bible teaches us about the "fear of God". Unfortunately, many people assume that we are to have a literal fear or terror, of God. Logic would teach us that God does not want us to be terrified of Him. I definitely do not want my children to be terrified of me. We run from whatever we fear. God certainly does not want us to run from Him. In fact, conversely, He said if we will run to Him, (draw nigh to Him), He will run to us.

There are two basic types of fear. The one, which we have already mentioned, is terror. The other is respect. Proper use of power brings respect. Abuse of power brings fear. The fear of God is a healthy respect for His authority and His power. We should never be afraid of Him or of approaching Him.

I know so many Christians, who love God with all their heart, and would never think of committing any gross act of sin. Yet they think nothing of feeding their fear stronghold on a constant basis. You can't talk to them for more than five minutes without hearing some hint of fear in what they are saying. We need to recognize fear as an enemy to God's kingdom in our lives. Anything which establishes a stronghold in my life is God's enemy.

Let's get back to the guy with the fear stronghold, criticizing the one with the lust stronghold. The man with the lust problem looks at the one with fear, almost in envy. He says, "I wish I had a fear stronghold instead of a lust stronghold. Then I would quit doing what I keep doing all the time. Oh, yes, I might sit in a corner and shake from fear, but at least I wouldn't keep sinning like this."

The one with the fear stronghold says, "I wish I had a lust stronghold instead of a fear stronghold. This fear paralyzes me! If my problem was lust, I would just quit doing it!" Now there's a thought! I am certain the guy with the lust stronghold never thought of that! That's the solution. Quit doing it.......Get real! You don't understand his stronghold any more than he understands yours. They are both displeasing to God (both in rebellion against God's authority), and both started when each of you voted in your thought life.

Of course, the guy with the pride stronghold says, "Neither one of you know what you're talking about!" He is in the deepest trouble! Remember, the most dangerous enemy is the one you cannot see. All he notices is the weakness of the other two. He doesn't see what is wrong within himself.

Please understand; you are not limited to only one type of stronghold in your life. Some of us excel in strongholds! We stretch above average; we have more than one stronghold! Remember, child of God, you can have anything you want!

The bottom line is that we need to be compassionate regarding each other's strongholds. You may not fully understand the reasons behind another person's struggle, but you can still empathize with them, while being mindful of your own battle with other strongholds.

When Israel was released from Babylonian captivity, they returned to the ruins of Jerusalem. The city they loved had been destroyed by their enemies. Their homes, shops, the Temple, and even the walls of the city had been destroyed. It was time to rebuild, to regain what they once had.

They immediately set about the task of reconstructing the Temple. It took approximately 20 years for them to rebuild the Temple. Seventy years after the Temple had been rebuilt, (ninety years after their release from captivity), along comes a man by the name of Nehemiah. He said (paraphrased), "It is wonderful that you fixed the Temple, but have you noticed our walls?"

Nothing had been done for the crumbling walls. All of their attention had been focused on the Temple. Nehemiah explained to them that without the walls, the Temple was vulnerable. Rebuilding the Temple established relationship with God. Rebuilding the walls established defense against their enemies.

When we fail God and allow ourselves to be carried away into captivity, we come back home longing for a renewal of that relationship. We focus all of our attention on the Temple. We re-establish relationship with God. The mistake we make is that, like Israel, we forget the walls. True, we have relationship with God, but that relationship (temple) is vulnerable because of the lack of defense (walls).

If we compare Israel to our own lives, we can compare our spirit to the temple. Our soul (our mind, will and emotions) is the walls.

Our body is the country of Israel surrounding Jerusalem. When we ask Jesus to come into our heart (spirit), we often forget to deal with the soul. We fail to establish His Lordship in our emotions, our thoughts, our attitudes, our habits, our relationships, our motives, our past, our failures, our hurts, our future, our career, our finances, and our family - all of the areas within our soul. If you think about it, these are the areas in our lives, which were devastated while we were in captivity to satan. The walls were broken down - destroyed.

Coming to God and establishing a spiritual relationship with Him does not immediately assure us of the healing of the walls (our soul). Don't assume that because you have prayed the sinner's prayer, all of your emotional and mental hurts have automatically been healed. In Romans 12:2 and Ephesians 4:23, we are told of the importance of renewing our mind. This refers to the rebuilding of the walls in our soul.

As I previously stated, we should never assume that God's blessing in one realm of our life, indicates His approval in every area. When our temple has been rebuilt, we are blessed there. Unfortunately, we assume this means that all of Jerusalem is safe. Let me introduce myself; I am your Nehemiah. God sent me to tell you to check your walls. It does not matter how blessed you are in the temple, I want to know about your walls. Is Jesus the King of your soul, and not just your spirit?

Let's look at 2 Corinthians 10:6. In this passage Paul says that we will be ready to revenge all disobedience when our obedience is fulfilled. What is he really saying to us?

Typically, when someone speaks of the enemy, Christians think of one enemy (singular), satan. Let's think again. How many kings are there in this world? Three: God, satan and self. How many kingdoms did Jesus tell us to seek in Matthew 6:33? One:

the Kingdom of God. If there are three kings, and we are seeking one kingdom, how many enemies are there against God's kingdom? The obvious answer is two: satan and self.

It is imperative that we view self as an enemy to the Kingdom of God, not merely an innocent bystander. Self is not only a participant; self is the one who did the voting that established your stronghold in the first place. Every time self votes, you weaken the walls.

When Paul says we will be ready to revenge disobedience, he is actually saying that we will be ready to attack satan. This will only be true "when our obedience is fulfilled" - when we have conquered self. Simply stated, we will be ready to attack satan when we have conquered self.

As we look at the whole armor of God in Ephesians 6, we note that the first five pieces of armor are for protection, and only the last piece is for fighting. Study those first five pieces closely. Their purpose is to protect the soul. Putting on those five pieces of armor basically rebuilds the walls, providing defense against the enemy of our soul. Only after we have put on the protective armor (submitted in our soul) does He tell us to attack the enemy, using the sword of the Spirit.

In my opinion, we should spend five times as much time conquering self as we do attacking satan. Why is self such a formidable foe? Because he has been with you all of your life. Remember, your most dangerous enemy is the one you can't see.

Satan wants us to believe he's our only enemy. As we concentrate on attacking him, we fail to put on the protective armor. When we fight without armor, we are warring without protection. Remember, warfare means "You shoot - and they shoot back".

In 2 Corinthians 10:4, Paul says that the weapons of our warfare are not carnal. Of the three kings, God, satan, and self, who is carnal? The only carnal king is self. Paul is not warning us against the use of satan's weapons in warfare. He knows we won't do that. He is warning us that we should not go into battle with the weapons of self. You may say, "I would never do that." But we do, every time we vote in battle. Remember, every time you vote, you are peeling off armor, making yourself vulnerable.

A stronghold must be dismantled brick by brick. To do this, we must repent.

"Mark, I just want to thank you so much!! It was your words, faith, and inspiration that brought me back to God! I can never say thank you enough! After several years of pushing Him aside I realize now that the panic attacks that I have suffered were God's way of telling me to wake up!!! Thank you again for all you do."
R. S. FROM MICHIGAN

CHAPTER FOUR

Forgiveness

In the last several years, the body of Christ has come into a greater awareness of spiritual warfare. When I was younger, we didn't hear much talk of warfare, other than a passing comment, in regard to the spiritual life. One day God showed me that because satan is threatened by the increase of warfare activity in Christian ranks, he will now intensify the use of one of his most effective weapons. God said, "In the next few years, notice the increase in frustration between Christians. Satan knows that your weapons are greater than his. You have bigger guns. If you are in a warfare mode, shooting at him, his only hope of survival is to get you to shoot in a different direction. He will do everything he can to cause Christians to offend other Christians, so you'll stop shooting at him and start aiming at your brothers and sisters in Christ."

Did you ever see the old black and white movies in which the "bad guy" is running from the cops? Usually he will end up in a deserted warehouse, hiding behind some crates. When the police enter the warehouse and tell him he's surrounded, you will often see him pick up something lying on the floor. It may be a bottle, a pipe or a rock. He throws the object to draw away their attention. Notice, he doesn't throw it straight up in the air. He throws it to the opposite side of the warehouse, so they will shoot in a different direction. This is what satan does when he gets us at odds with our Christian brothers and sisters. He gets us to shoot in their direction, so we won't be shooting at him.

God has a number of laws which work all the time - 24 hours a day - 365 days a year. They work for Christians as well as sinners. One of them is the law of gravity. Gravity does not work only on certain days or for certain people. If it only worked for Christians, we wouldn't even need discerning of spirits to know who was unsaved. They'd be floating.

Sometimes God's laws work for you, and other times they work against you, depending on whether or not you are cooperating with them. Gravity is a blessing when I set a glass on a table. I know it won't float away when I let go; it will stay right there. Sometimes, however, we may slip or stumble, and find gravity working against us. It's not that gravity has something against you personally. Gravity does not have a mind of its own. It does one thing, and it does it well; it pulls everything toward the center of the earth.

Another of God's laws is the law of agreement. Matthew 18:19 says that if two agree about anything we ask, it will be done. Our strength is in unity. We've all heard the great quote by Martin Luther, "United we stand, divided we fall." Even Jesus, in Matthew 12:25, stated that a house divided against itself cannot stand.

In Genesis 11, we read the story of the tower of Babel. This is the story of a group of ungodly people who determined in their hearts to build a tower unto themselves. In verse 6, God makes a remarkable statement about these wicked people. He said that because the people were of one mind, nothing would be impossible to them. Imagine that! When wicked people are in unity, nothing can stop them. In fact, look at what God did to defeat them. He changed their languages, to destroy that unity. What a lesson to us for our marriages, our families, and other relationships. When communication is interrupted, unity is weakened.

Think of the millions of dollars spent by governments throughout the world in their efforts to obliterate organized crime. Why have they been unsuccessful? The answer is unity. In organized crime, a person takes an oath of allegiance, loyalty to an organization, or crime family. As Genesis 11:6 states, because they are of one mind, nothing can stop them.

Deuteronomy 32:30 tells of the potential strength in unity. It states that if one can put a thousand to flight, two can put ten thousand to flight. Logic would tell us that two could put two thousand to flight. Why does the Bible say ten thousand? Because, when we are in unity, our strength multiplies exponentially.

Satan knows this principle. In response, he does everything possible to keep us out of unity. He incites dramatic division in the Christian ranks by pointing out the differences in our denominational and theological beliefs. There are, sadly enough, some Christian organizations that exist for the sole purpose of fault-finding - pointing out any and every difference in the body of Christ - hindering unity. If, by chance, you have purchased a book written by such people, let me ask you a question. How many people came to Christ as a result of that organization in the past year? Then ask yourself, how many came to Christ through those ministries that are being criticized?

Some of my closest friends in ministry have beliefs which are different from mine. But we have more in common than in difference. If you believe that Jesus is the only Son of God who was born of a virgin, lived a sinless life, died on a cross, and bodily rose again, I think we have a lot in common. I must tell you that I would not give one cent in support of a "ministry" that criticizes or brings division to the body of Christ. This does not mean that we should close our eyes to obvious doctrinal error, which could potentially endanger someone's eternal soul. I find, however, that most of the discussion on our difference in beliefs centers on different styles of worship, etc., which I do not believe to have an effect on where that person will spend eternity. After all, isn't eternity the real issue?

Israel was comprised of twelve distinctly different tribes. Each tribe had its own peculiarities which differentiated that tribe from the other eleven. Though they were different, they were in unity in two areas: worship and warfare. They had the same God and the same enemy. If we have the same God and the same enemy, we can fight side by side - not face to face.

Matthew 18:15-17 details God's prescription for healing an offense between brothers. The sole intent in this passage is to aid us in establishing and maintaining unity in the body of Christ. The next verse, Matthew 18:18 contains a principle with which we are all familiar: "Whatever we bind on earth will be bound in heaven and whatever we loose on earth will be loosed in heaven." This is another of God's laws - the law of binding and loosing.

I've wondered why Jesus stated the same principle twice. He didn't often do this. Notice that Matthew 16:19 is almost exactly the same as Matthew 18:18. Both of these verses state the "law of binding and loosing". But why is it stated twice in the same book?

If you recall, I mentioned previously that God's laws work for us and against us, depending on whether we cooperate with them. In Matthew 16, Jesus is speaking to His disciples, handing them the keys of the kingdom. He reveals that as a result of this they can bind and loose, obviously stating the benefit of this law for those who cooperate with it.

In Matthew 18, however, I believe Jesus is warning us of the potential danger when we do not cooperate with this law. Basically, I believe He is saying in verses 15-17, that we should make peace with our brother at any cost. Then, in verse 18, He tells the penalty for not doing this. If we stay out of unity, and refuse to forgive, we have bound (tied) our own hands in regard to spiritual warfare. When we make peace with our brother and forgive him, we "loose" our hands for spiritual warfare.

In verse 19, He continues with the theme of unity by saying that if we are in agreement, our prayers will be answered. It is obvious to me that there could be only one reason for sandwiching the law of "binding and loosing" between these passages on forgiveness and unity. When I forgive my brother, I am removing the ropes from my hands - bonds placed there by me when I first decided to hold a grudge.

In verse 21 of that same chapter, Peter continues the theme on unity by asking how often he should forgive his brother for the same sin. In the law, they were taught to forgive a brother seven times in the same day for the same sin. When Peter inquired about this, Jesus used hyperbole to show Peter how ridiculous it is to place a limit on the number of times we should forgive someone, by saying seventy times seven. I do not believe Jesus was actually saying that we should even limit our forgiveness to 490 times per day. If you calculate it out, that's approximately once every three minutes. Basically, Jesus was saying that we should forgive our brother as often as is necessary to keep our hands free in warfare.

A few years ago, someone asked me how he could forgive someone he did not trust. I explained to him that it is not necessary to trust someone in order to forgive them. Don't let people manipulate you with the statement, "If you really forgive me, you'll trust me."

Think about it. Why does the bank forgive a loan? It's because they don't believe you will ever pay it back. To get it off their books, they will sometimes forgive it. After that loan is forgiven, do you still owe them anything? The answer is "no". Now, do you think they will loan you money again? Absolutely not! They have forgiven you, but they don't trust you.

To prove that we have forgiven the bank robber, is it necessary that we make him a teller? If we have forgiven the terrorist, must we prove it by making him the head of airport security?

Forgiveness is not a "one time" thing. It is a lifetime commitment. Have you noticed that sometimes you will think you've totally won the victory over bitterness, and when you least expect it, that memory comes back to haunt you? When it does, you must forgive again. It's amazing how little it may take to trigger the memory of the pain, a mention of the name or even the smell of the cologne the person wears. When something reminds you, and irritation re-surfaces, it's time to forgive again - seventy times seven - 490 times a day - once every three minutes! That means that at most, you can only hold a grudge for two minutes and fifty nine seconds!

A while back I did a study of the conscious and subconscious mind. The subconscious stores everything that we have ever experienced. As I mentioned earlier, by age 30, it has stored more than three trillion memories. I once read that one of the character-istics of the subconscious is that it cannot distinguish emotionally between a real experience and an imagined one. This is why the Bible says (in Matthew 5:28) that if a man lusts after a woman, he has already committed adultery with her in his heart. Although he may not have even touched her, his subconscious mind has expe-rienced similar emotions, to those he would experience if he had actually committed adultery with her.

There are individuals who will tell you every painful thing they have ever encountered, if you'll just sit and listen long enough. What they do not realize is that they are causing themselves to experience the pain one more time. Every time you relive an experience in your mind, your subconscious assumes it is happening to you again. Why would you allow anyone to hurt you again?

The way I see it, the reason I forgive is because I love myself too much to let me go through that pain again, not to mention the fact that God voted in favor of forgiveness. If we don't forgive, who voted?

When we hold a grudge, we are removing the breastplate of righteousness from our emotions, and leaving them vulnerable to satan and his demons.

Forgiveness is a process, not an experience. Ask the Holy Spirit to help you walk through the forgiveness process. Your healing will come as you forgive. And, until you submit this part of your emotions to God, you are not wearing the "whole armor of God" – you're not ready for battle.

"We are just a little fish in this big pond, but you have given so much to help us - not only in our business, but in our personal spiritual walk as well. It's refreshing to be with others who recognize that these "parts" of our lives were never meant to be compartmentalized."

L. O. FROM TEXAS

CHAPTER 5

The Glory Of God

In the sixth chapter of Ephesians, God gives us weapons for warfare, but I can't find where God describes weapons for himself. The reason is that He doesn't need any. God's glory defeats all of His enemies.

The glory of God is the manifestation of His presence. God's glory is a part of His Being. Because of this, His glory is wherever He is.

When Jesus prayed in the garden in John 17:5 (NIV), He said, "And now, Father, glorify Me in Your presence with the glory I had with You before the world began." After praying this, He met soldiers who were coming to arrest Him. He asked for whom were they looking, and they answered, "Jesus of Nazareth." When He said this, what happened to the soldiers? They fell backwards.

What caused them to fall backwards? Did Jesus strike them or attack them? No! They were smitten by His glory.

In 2 Thessalonians 2:8, we are told that when Jesus returns He will destroy His enemies. How will He destroy them? What weapon will He use? He will not use any weapons. We are told that they will be destroyed by the "brightness of His coming." What is this brightness? It's His glory. In fact, Habakkuk 3:3-4 says, "...His glory covered the heavens, and the earth was full of His praise. And His brightness was as the light..."

When Moses was called by God to go up to Mount Sinai, the Bible says that the appearance of the glory of the Lord on Mount Sinai was like a fire. Moses asked God to allow him to see His glory. God cautioned Moses, telling him that no man could see His face and live. However, He tempered this by telling Moses to hide in the cleft of the rock as He passed by. God covered him with His hand as He passed by, and allowed Moses to see only the after-glow of His glory. When Moses came down from the mountain after being in God's presence, his face shone so brightly with the glory of God that he had to wear a veil so people could look at him without being blinded by God's glory.

If God's glory defeats all of His enemies, and if His glory is His presence, then all He must do to win any battle is show up! When did God win? As soon as He arrived.

You and I must come to the place that we understand that God's glory is our only source of victory. We don't have several options. It is our only source. And remember, the original Greek for "only" is "only".

One may say, "I thought the Word of God was a source of victory." Without God's glory, anointing and empowering it, the Bible would be just another book.

Others may say, "The Name of Jesus is a source of victory." The reason that Name is above every other name is because His glory is attached to it. If I hear one of my children call me from another part of the house, and if there is an urgency in the word "Daddy", I will immediately rush to them. When we speak the Name of Jesus, He comes on the scene. Speaking that Name brings His glory.

When Jesus was teaching the disciples how to pray, He taught us that the solution to all of the problems in this world is contained in one thing: "Thy kingdom come...on earth." Why was this so important? Because God is a monarch. He is a King. Where do kings dwell? In their own kingdom.

When we need victory, we need God's glory. God's glory is His presence, so it can only be found where He is. He is in His kingdom; so the obvious need is for His kingdom to be established anywhere I need victory.

Remember the definition of a kingdom: "A kingdom is any place where the king's authority is obeyed without question and without hesitation." In a kingdom, only one person votes. If you want to know who the king is, find out who is voting.

This is why Jesus said that the solution for everything in this world is, "Thy kingdom come."

When the earth was in its worst chaotic mess, what did God use to "clean it up"? Genesis 1:2 says that God's Spirit brought order out of chaos. His presence - His glory brought order to the earth.

After that time, His glory remained on the earth. When Adam and Eve were created, they were created in His glory. They lived in His glory. There were no problems on the earth at that time. Why? Think about it! There were no hurricanes, tornadoes, earthquakes, or famines. There was no disease, pain, rape, incest, alcoholism, drug addiction, hatred, violence or murder. Why?

Before God created Adam, He was the King of the earth. After creating Adam, God made him king of the earth. He gave him dominion over the earth and everything in it.

At that time, Adam remained submitted to God. When a king submits himself to another king, he gives that king authority over his kingdom. Although the earth was technically Adam's kingdom, by submitting to God, he made it God's Kingdom. Because of this, God's glory remained on the earth and defeated any enemies which would have caused hurt to Adam and Eve.

The obvious question is, if this were true, how did satan have access to Adam and Eve in the form of a serpent? God allowed satan to approach them and communicate with them, but he was not allowed to harm them. Why would He do this? God doesn't want robots which are programmed to love Him and honor Him. He wants us to serve Him because we choose to do so. The only way we could have a choice is if God allowed a second option to be presented to us. The serpent was permitted to go into the garden so that man could choose.

As long as Adam and Eve remained submitted to God, maintaining His Kingship on the earth, there were no problems. When satan tempted them to sin, his goal was much greater than the loss of Adam's or Eve's souls. He knew that because the entire earth was under their dominion, as long as they were submitted to God, he could not harm the earth because it was protected by God's glory. He needed to get rid of God's glory. The only way to achieve that was to crown a new king. He needed Adam to vote.

Several years ago, I heard a minister on television say, "When Adam bowed down and worshipped satan..." Did I miss a verse? As far as I know, Adam never worshipped satan. When the serpent approached Eve, he didn't say, "I have this new concept. Tell me what you think about it. I was thinking, perhaps, you could bow down and worship me. You could offer animal sacrifices; we would have heavy metal music in the background, burn black candles, and I would draw a pentagram on the ground. We would call it satanic worship. What do you think?"

Numerous Christians think that the only way satan comes

against us is by saying, "Do you want to sin? Come here for a minute and I'll show you how." He is much more cunning than that.
Satan's desire for every Christian is that you have a promotion.
He wants you to be king of your life. If you are king, God's glory
moves out and satan has access to your kingdom.

Satan does not fear all Christians - only submitted Christians.
In reality, the only thing he fears is God's glory. And the only
Christians who are filled with God's glory are those who have sub-
mitted themselves fully to Him. They are filled with His kingdom.

The serpent approached Eve and remarked, "You know, you have
real leadership potential." (paraphrased) Eve replied, "Yes! I receive
that!" (Just because a "word" sounds good, that is no indication that
it came from the Lord. Be careful!)

The serpent then commented, "I believe you could run this place."
Eve replied, "You know, you're very perceptive." He then said, "You
should be king." In actuality, in Genesis 3:5, he stated, "...and ye
shall be as gods..."

When Adam and Eve voted, they suddenly felt naked. Why
didn't they feel naked before? I believe that prior to this time, they
had been clothed with God's glory. It was not until God's glory
lifted from the earth that they felt naked.

I believe there are two reasons why God's glory was removed
from the earth at that time. First, He was no longer the king. Since
this was not His kingdom, and because He only dwells in His kingdom, He "moved out". The second reason brings sadness. God had
created man for fellowship. Now, if He were to come near them,
His glory would kill them. You see, there was sin in them, and sin
is an enemy of God. Because His glory destroys His enemies, it
would have destroyed the sin in Adam and Eve, and by so doing,
they would have been destroyed as well. God could not separate
Himself from His glory. He could not set His glory on a shelf

while He visited with man. His glory is His presence. Therefore, He would have to love them from a distance.

What now? How will God bring healing to this dilemma?

We find His solution in Exodus 25:22, when Moses was building the Ark of the Covenant for the Tabernacle. Remember, the ark represented God's glory. Above the ark were two cherubims - symbols of His glory. In Exodus 25:22, God announced, "And there I will meet with thee and I will commune with thee from above the mercy seat, from between the two cherubims, which are on the ark of the testimony, of all things which I will give thee in commandment unto the children of Israel."

What a wonderful solution! Since God cannot separate Himself from His glory, He coupled His glory with mercy. The cherubims represented God's glory, and they sat above the "mercy seat". Basically, God said, "Where My glory meets mercy, I will meet with you." The only thing that protects sinful man from being destroyed by God's glory is His mercy.

Inside the ark was the law which had been broken by man. Isn't it wonderful that God placed, not the judgment seat, but the mercy seat above the law! Now, in order to look upon the law which had been broken by man, God must look through mercy.

Understand, they could not meet with God just anywhere. They could only meet with Him above the mercy seat. If you could go back in time to those days and ask one of the children of Israel where God is, he would probably say something like this: "Go down to the end of this row of tents. Hang a right. Proceed to the end of that row of tents. Look off to your left. You will see a big tabernacle there. Go through the front entrance. He's not there, but you are getting warm. That is the outer court. Now go into the inner court. You are getting warmer. You will then see a veil. Don't go past the veil. Trust me! You do not want to go past the veil.

But if you could, you would find a gold box. God is in that box."
That was the only place they could meet with God.

With this new-found way of coming into God's presence, not
everyone was granted that privilege. Only one man could enter
once a year. On the day of Atonement, the high priest went in to
the Holy of Holies. When he entered, he had a rope tied around
his ankle, with bells dangling from the bottom of his garment. You
may ask, "Why?" You see, if there was any sin in his life, he would
be killed as he entered God's presence. That is why he needed the
rope and the bells. He had to keep moving the entire time he was
in there, so they could hear the bells, which signified that he was
still alive. If the bells stopped ringing, no one else could go in to the
Holy of Holies. They had to pull him out by the rope.

The obvious question is that if God's glory was coupled with
mercy, why would someone be killed in His presence? I personally
believe it is because the blood that was sprinkled upon the mercy
seat was from a lamb, not from Jesus – the perfect Lamb of God.
Now that His blood is sprinkled upon our hearts, we can come into
God's presence with no fear.

"Thank you for your wonderful ministry. I have enjoyed… been challenged by… and been richly blessed by your ministry. I have long admired your humor, your teaching, your leadership, and your openness to be used by God's Holy Spirit. From the first time I heard you speak, through tapes, and now on CD… I have felt God's spirit touch my heart. More often than not, I am moved to share my notes with others, or pass along the CD of the month. You move in wider circles than you know."

D. H. FROM CALIFORNIA

CHAPTER 6

THE LOSS OF GOD'S GLORY

As long as the Israelites had the Ark, they won their battles. It seemed that they just couldn't lose. Have you noticed that when everything seems to be going your way, you have a tendency to get a bit presumptuous? We begin to think that we are invincible. We start believing our own press release. Just a hint... You're in trouble!

The Israelites thought they had God in a box.

Eventually, they started scrutinizing God's management policies, presuming they had a license to critique His decisions. After a while, perhaps someone said, "I foresee that I could run this part of the kingdom better than it's being handled now." (I think the "new agers" call this "self-empowerment". God calls it rebellion.)

Bit by bit, the people began taking back the kingdom from God by voting and establishing themselves as kings. Eventually, they gave God the ultimate insult. They said, "Let's make it official. God, give us a man to be king over us." Why did they need a man to be king over them? God had been their king. He had never abused His authority. He protected them and provided for them. He was kind and generous. Why did they want a man?

God gave them a man. He gave them King Self... I mean, King Saul.

Before Saul became king, however, they lost the box (the ark). What I am actually concluding is that they lost the glory.

Israel was in a war with the Philistines. When the Israelites began to lose, they became nervous. You see, they weren't good at losing. They had always won. "How could this be? We still have God's box."

"Well, somebody go get him!"

"Get who?"

"Get God!"

"Where is God?"

"He is in His box!"

"Which box?"

"God's box!" "Somebody come help me!"

"Where are you going?"

"To retrieve God's box. He is too heavy for me!" (I'm not sure, but this may not have been the exact conversation. We call this speculation.)

The amazing thing is that they broke twenty-eight laws by going into the Holy of Holies and taking the Ark. Can you believe that no one died in the process? Of course they didn't! It wasn't the Ark that could kill them. It was God's glory and He had already departed.

Those were the laws of the previous king, so they didn't matter now.

What they took to the battlefield was not God. It was just a box. True, it was the Ark of the Covenant, and it contained the tablets of the law, but what they needed wasn't law -- they needed God. Can we learn something from this? Why do we feel so secure with our rules and regulations? The Ten Commandments in a gold box could not save Israel. What makes you think your laws and regulations will save you?

When they lost the battle, the Philistines took the Ark. They took it to the city of Ashdod and set it up in the temple of Dagon, their false god. When they came back the next day, Dagon had fallen flat on his face. (Why did this happen? The only thing I can guess is that somewhere along the way, after the Ark left Israel, God's glory rejoined the ark.)

They set Dagon upright, leaving this false god in the presence of the only true God. The next morning, Dagon had fallen again. His head and hands were cut off. God sent a plague of tumors on the city of Ashdod, so they sent the Ark to Gath. This city also was plagued with tumors.

They then sent the Ark to Ekron. The city was in a panic. Many of the people died, and those who survived were afflicted with tumors.

After keeping the Ark for seven months, the Philistines had encountered enough troubles. They set it on a new cart hitched to two cows and sent it back to Israel.

When the people of Bethshemesh saw the Ark, they stopped harvesting their wheat and rejoiced at the sight of it. 1 Sam. 6:14 (NIV) says: "...the people chopped up the wood of the cart and sacrificed the cows as a burnt offering to the Lord."

Then, for some reason, they became curious. They opened the Ark to look inside. Remember, the lid of the Ark was the Mercy Seat. To look inside the Ark, they separated mercy from God's glory. At that moment, being exposed to God's glory without mercy, they died. When this happened, they took the Ark into the home of Abinadab. His son, Eleazar, was consecrated to look after the Ark. The Ark remained there for 20 years. During this time much of Israel continued to serve false gods and, as a consequence, they eventually asked God to give them a man to be king over them.

It is sad to note that as long as Saul was king, he never sought to bring the Ark back to its proper place. Isn't that like self? When self is king, we may go through the motions, but we don't really want to put God in His proper place in our lives.

On one occasion God told Saul to destroy the Amalekites. He told him to kill everything that breathed. Now that's not hard to understand. All you do is take a pocket mirror, put it under the nearest nose, if it fogs up... KILL!

Saul made an executive decision. (Only kings make executive decisions, so we know that God wasn't king.) Saul decided to keep the livestock alive. He would have been the hero of all the animal rights activists. When he walked into the room they would have played "Born Free".

He brought the animals back to Israel. When the prophet, Samuel, approached him, he asked if Saul had obeyed the word of the Lord. Saul immediately said, "Oh, yeah, I'm submitted." So Samuel asked why he could hear the bleating of sheep.

You have to give Saul credit. He was smooth! He could make up a lie at the drop of a hat. He told Samuel that he was planning to sacrifice those animals to God. Well, that was not true. If he were going to do that, he would have done it on the battlefield.

He was going to have a barbecue. His wife was probably at home, making potato salad.

Samuel's next statement to Saul is a kingdom principle. "To obey is better than sacrifice." Why is obedience greater than sacrifice? Because sacrifice does not characterize a kingdom. Only one thing constitutes a kingdom: obedience. This is why tithing is greater than fasting. Fasting is sacrifice, but tithing is obedience.

Eventually, Israel had a king after God's own heart -- David. In David's first official statement as king, in 1 Chronicles 13:3, he said, "Let us bring again the Ark of our God to us; for we inquired not at it in the days of Saul." What a sad testimony to Saul's reign, that he was remembered as the king who did not seek God.

In Psalm 132: 3-5, David vowed that he would not rest until he found a dwelling place for God.

Two kings: Saul and David. One was eulogized as the man after God's own heart; the other, as the man who did not go after the Ark. At one point, God even told the prophet not to pray for him anymore. It is interesting to note that one of these men was guilty of adultery and murder. He broke two of the Ten Commandments. The other refused to kill some animals.

How could an adulterous murderer be known as a man after God's own heart? How could a man who wanted to "save the animals" be known as a "lost cause"?

I believe the answer is found in this; when David was confronted with his sin, he readily admitted, "I am that man." When Saul was confronted, however, he denied his wrongful acts emphatically.

We have all had moments of failure -- times when we have rebelled against God's authority -- voted. The key to survival is for you, when confronted with your sin, to be quick to submit. In God's eyes, Saul's haughty stubbornness and self-righteousness was worse than David's sin of adultery and murder. Why?

As I told you previously, pride is the most dangerous of all strongholds. Saul could have looked down his nose at David's stronghold of lust, thinking himself better because he had never committed such vile sins. All sins stink in God's nostrils. Sometimes I wonder if those with strongholds of lust are safer than those with pride. They can see their enemy more easily, and hopefully, they will quickly repent.

"I just have to let ya'll know how much God has blessed me, especially after this weekend. I have never enjoyed hearing anyone speak on life and its circumstances as much as I did Mark this weekend! I laughed so hard...and my heart was moved at the same time. I have found a new hero. Thank you."

N. P. FROM ALABAMA

CHAPTER 7

RESTORING GOD'S GLORY

Davi's first order of business was to bring home the Ark. In 1 Chronicles 13, the story unfolds. David assembled the Israelites and proceeded to the house of Abinadab, where the Ark had been kept for the past 20 years. They set the Ark on a new cart, pulled by oxen.

Understand how thrilled they were to finally see God's glory restored to Israel. They were celebrating with music and instruments as they followed the Ark. When they came to the threshing floor of Chidon, the oxen stumbled. Uzza, one of the young men who was driving the cart, reached up and grabbed the Ark to stabilize it - to keep it from falling. He was killed immediately.

For years this story has frustrated me. I said, "God, why would you kill him? He was just protecting your box." It wasn't until I studied a bit further that I learned what I believe to be the reason for this.

Abinadab had more than one son. His son, Eleazar, had been

consecrated to care for the Ark while it was in his home. Uzza was also his son. More than likely, growing up in the home that housed the Ark, Uzza began to think of it as just another piece of furniture. He probably viewed the Ark as a coffee table or a credenza. Unfortunately all too often, those of us, who have grown up around the things of God, the presence of God, the moving of God, begin to think of them as common. This is a dangerous and presumptuous mistake.

In the original Hebrew, the name Uzza means "strength" or "the strength of man". Here we see the strength of man saying, "Oh, that's just the glory of God. My strength can handle that. Watch me salvage God's glory." After learning this, I found it easier to accept what happened.

After this incident, David stopped the procession, and returned home. In 1 Chronicles 13:12 (NIV), David said, "How can I ever bring the ark of God to me." Instead of taking the Ark to Jerusalem, they put it in the house of Obed-Edom. It remained there for three months. Verse 14 says that the Lord blessed his household and everything he had while the Ark was there.

Do you realize why we are studying this story? This is not a history lesson. I believe that God is wanting to do again in the earth, what David did in Israel. He desires to restore His glory – to bring back the glory.

Jesus prayed a prayer that has not yet been answered. In the Lord's Prayer, He said, "Thy kingdom come...on earth." You may be saying, "But that's not an accurate quotation because you took out some of the words in the middle of His statement." Let's look at what was left out. In actuality, Jesus said, "Thy kingdom come, Thy will be done, on earth as it is in heaven." The spirit of the statement is the same, regardless. Jesus wants God's kingship to be established on earth. If God is the king, it follows that His Will be done. That is what happens in a kingdom. The second phrase, "Thy Will be done" helps us to understand the first phrase, "Thy kingdom come".

Now, let us get back to the issue of the prayer that has not yet been answered. From the time Jesus prayed that prayer until now, God has not been the king of the earth. You may say, "How do you know?" It's simple. In a kingdom, only one person votes. That is the way you know who the king is. Can we honestly look at the world around us and say that God has voted for everything that is happening? Obviously not!

The mistake some people have made, in teaching the establishment of God's kingdom on the earth, is in the assumption that we must concern ourselves with the physical aspects of God's kingdom. When the spiritual part is right -- when God is king in our lives, it follows that He will automatically be king over our physical possessions as well. If God is the king of my life, and I am submitted to Him, He is also king of everything I own, including my home and the land on which it sits.

In 1 Chronicles 15:2, David realized the mistake he had made previously. He said, "None ought to carry the Ark of God but the Levites: for them hath the Lord chosen to carry the Ark of God, and to minister unto Him forever." The mistake they had made was in placing God's glory on a cart with oxen. Where did they get this idea? From the ungodly Philistines.

In 1 Chronicles 15:13(NIV), David said "It was because you, the Levites, did not bring it up the first time that the Lord, our God, broke out in anger against us. We did not inquire of Him about how to do it in the prescribed way."

God created man for fellowship. God wants His glory to rest on the priests, the Levites. Who are the priests? 1 Peter 2:9 tells us that we are a royal priesthood. God wants His glory to rest upon us. As God restores His glory to this earth, He will move upon and through us, His priests.

In 1 Chronicles 15:12, David told the priests to sanctify themselves before they brought the Ark back to Jerusalem. Basically, he was telling them to make sure that they were submitted to God, and that their hearts were right before God, so that His glory (the Ark) could rest upon their shoulders.

David went to great lengths to prepare musicians and singers, so they could offer up praises as the glory was being restored to Israel. He was so jubilant, that he began to dance before the Lord. When his wife, Michal, saw him dancing, the Bible says she despised him in her heart.

I was brought up in a church environment in which we believed in many of the things of God, which other Christians dismissed. I was taught about the baptism in the Holy Spirit with the evidence of speaking in other tongues, the laying on of hands, being slain in the Spirit, miracles, divine healing, signs and wonders. It was not uncommon in our church for God to speak to a minister and give him insight, which enabled him to minister to a person through the gift of the word of knowledge, the word of wisdom or the word of prophecy. On many occasions I have seen my dad and others speak to an individual in a service, and tell them things about their life that no one knew. It had to be God! As I started in ministry, I asked God to use me in this same way. Now ministering in this way, in the gifts of the Spirit, is an integral part of my ministry.

Isn't it amazing that we all think we are open to anything that is of God when, in reality, we only accept the things of God with which we are familiar. This is called having our loins girt about with tradition.

All my life I was told that if you dance in church, you had better be dancing in the Spirit. My concept of dancing in the Spirit was that a person, when worshipping God, would suddenly break forth in dance with little or no awareness of what was happening to them. Later someone would inform them that they had danced in the Spirit.

The Bible does not say that David danced in the Spirit. In 2 Samuel 6:14 it says "David danced before the Lord with all his might." In fact, of the 19 references to dance in the Bible, I can not find one verse which refers to 'dancing in the Spirit'. But that certainly didn't hinder our tradition.

In 1980, I was privileged to make my first ministry trip to Australia. I was a seasoned minister at the ripe old age of 22. While seated on the platform of Christian Life Center in Sydney, where Frank Houston was pastor, I was horrified as people began to dance during the time of worship. I knew they weren't dancing in the Spirit because their eyes were open. In my opinion, they were 'in the flesh'. What concerned me even more was the fact that this church belonged to the same denomination in which I had grown up. How could they be so different? I had a fleeting thought: Thank God they brought me in, just in the nick of time, to correct this error in their church!

Something began to happen in me as I continued to watch them dance before the Lord. True, they were cognizant of what they were doing, but I could see that their worship was real. They weren't doing this for themselves -- it was for the Lord. At that moment, I couldn't think of a scripture to back me up. All I knew was that I bore witness in my spirit that this was God and that He approved of what was taking place.

I looked around and didn't see anyone from home. My dad wasn't there. My district superintendent wasn't there, and I thought, "What they don't know won't hurt them." I started dancing too! It felt good. It felt right. I felt the presence of God.

In retrospect, I find it illogical that we would think that God wanted us to consciously choose to praise Him with our mouths and not with our feet.

I am prepared to admit that there are those who abuse the dance. In actuality, everything God does gets taken to the extreme by someone. The mistake we make is that we outlaw the moving of God in order to prevent it from being abused. In his book, A Tale of Three Kings, (which helped me survive one of the darkest hours in my life), Gene Edwards says, "Rules were invented by elders so they could get to bed early." It is much easier for us to outlaw something than it is to police it. Time and again the Bible tells us of praising the Lord with the dance. I see no scriptural basis to forbid it.

You might not be comfortable with dancing before the Lord. Please do not think I am saying you are required to dance. The Bible also says to sing unto the Lord, to play on the harp, the trumpet, the cymbals, and other instruments. We are not required to do any of these, but we have the liberty to do all of them.

There are denominations and organizations who have taken strong stands against dancing in the church. My caution to them is this -- remember the words of Gamaliel in Acts 5:38-39 (NRSV). He said, "I tell you, keep away from these men and let them alone; because if this plan or this undertaking is of human origin, it will fail; but if it is of God, you will not be able to overthrow them -- in that case you may even be found fighting against God!" (In light of the liberal criticism of some ministries today and of the manifestations taking place in revivals throughout the world, we should all take Gamaliel's advice. Let us be sure that something is not of God before we criticize it. Don't judge it with your tradition. Measure it against the truth of God's Word.)

Remember, David's wife Michal, who criticized him for dancing before the Lord, was childless. She never knew the joy of giving birth to a child. I fear for those who criticize others who rejoice in the dance as they experience God's glory. You may risk becoming spiritually barren.

If you enjoy the liberty of dancing before the Lord, may I caution you as well. Don't look down your nose at those who do not dance. As I said previously, we are not required to dance. I have seen some who have developed an attitude of supposed superiority because of their spiritual "enlightenment". Don't allow yourself to be lifted up in pride because of revelation God has given you. Make sure you are dancing to the right King.

Some have told me that they can accept "dancing before the Lord", but they have difficulty with the concept of people practicing and choreographing the dance. My question is "Aren't you glad the singers practice?" Is there any great merit to spontaneity? Why not give God our best?" Besides that, I have seen a few of you dance who could use the practice.

When the Ark returned to Jerusalem, it was not put back in its original place. Twenty years before, it had been taken from the Tabernacle of Moses, which sat on Mount Gibeon. It was now brought to Mount Zion, where David had prepared a new tabernacle.

After offering burnt sacrifices, David appointed priests to minister before the Ark. This was very unusual. In the Tabernacle of Moses, one man came before the Ark once a year. In David's tabernacle, however, all of the priests came before the Ark daily to offer sacrifices of praise and music.

Conversely, at Gibeon, they were still "going through the motions", offering burnt offerings in the Tabernacle of Moses.

The blood of animals was shed only once at David's tabernacle, once and for all. At Moses' tabernacle, blood was being shed again and again. Are you getting the picture? Hebrews 9:28 (NIV) says, "So Christ was sacrificed once to take away the sins of many people."

In Amos 9:11-12, God says, "In that day will I raise up the Tabernacle of David that is fallen, and close up the breaches thereof; and I will raise up his ruins, and I will build it as in the days of old: That they may possess the remnant of Edom, and of all the heathen, which are called by My Name, saith the Lord that doeth this."

In Acts chapter 15, we are told of a disagreement that was taking place in the church at Jerusalem. (I realize that it may be difficult to imagine a disagreement among Christians, but do your best.) There was a difference of opinion in regard to Gentiles having the right to be saved and baptized. It was basically segregation and discrimination in the church. Sound familiar?

In his argument on behalf of the Gentiles, James cited this prophecy from the Old Testament. In verses 16 and 17, he said, "After this, I will return, and will build again the Tabernacle of David, which is fallen down; and I will build again the ruins thereof, and I will set it up; That the residue of men might seek after the Lord, and all the Gentiles, upon whom My Name is called, saith the Lord, Who doeth all these things."

When the church leaders realized that the salvation of the Gentiles was part of the fulfillment of this prophecy, they came into agreement and accepted their Gentile brothers and sisters in Christ.

That prophecy is still being fulfilled today. God is restoring the Tabernacle of David. Extensive studies have been done on the Temple Mount in Jerusalem, with speculations as to when and how Solomon's temple would be rebuilt. I must admit that I do not have revelation regarding that; my concern is not so much with the physical building as it is with the spiritual Tabernacle of David.

In 2 Peter 1:13-14, Peter tells us that our body is a tabernacle. The actual Tabernacle of David was a tent; a temporary, movable dwelling place. Doesn't that describe our bodies?

I'm convinced that the restoration of the Tabernacle of David will not be accomplished with a physical tent, but will be a spiritual establishment, reviving us as tabernacles of praise.

Remember, David's tabernacle sat on Mount Zion. The body of Christ, His church, is spiritual Zion. The restoration of the Tabernacle of David is happening in us right now.

Hebrews 9:11-12 says, "But Christ, being come an High Priest of good things to come, by a greater and more perfect tabernacle, not made with hands, that is to say, not of this building; Neither by the blood of goats and calves, but by His own blood He entered in once into the holy place, having obtained eternal redemption for us."

God's glory was with the Ark in the Tabernacle of David; yet they continued with their tradition of blood sacrifices in Moses' tabernacle, even though the glory had been gone from there for twenty years. Does this sound like some of today's churches? Yes, the glory of God was once there. They had it. But, for whatever reason, it was lost. Yet churches continue to hold on to tradition, not realizing that their religious practice is just that...practice. "This is the way we've always done it. I don't know what they think they're doing over there, across town at that new place. We've been here longer than them. They're out of order."

In Isaiah 43:19, God says, "Behold, I will do a new thing; now it shall spring forth; shall ye not know it?" God asks if we will recognize the new things He is doing. I must admit that I "spit out" almost every new thing God sent into my life, before I realized it had been sent by God, and finally "swallowed it". Once again, I had my "loins girt about with tradition" instead of truth.

I had grown up around the moving of God's Spirit. I was filled with the Holy Spirit at age five. Praying in the Spirit, speaking in tongues, was a part of my life. When I was about sixteen years old I was sitting in a church service. The guest speaker, a powerful woman of God, told us that we should begin singing in the Spirit. I was horrified! You can't just choose to sing in the Spirit. It's sort of like dancing in the Spirit. Remember that? I figured God had to "sneak up on you" and sing through you without you knowing what was happening. Now this woman had the audacity to suggest that we sing in the Spirit of our own volition. What if God struck her with lightning? Thank God, I was sitting in the back of the church. (I had gotten there early so I could get a seat in the back of the building. If you don't get there early enough, the other Christians will beat you to it, and you'll end up having to sit in the front. If you didn't grow up in church, like me, you won't see the humor in this.)

Later, as I was reading in 1 Corinthians 14:15, Paul's words radiated, "What is it then? I will pray with the Spirit, and I will pray with the understanding also: I will sing with the Spirit, and I will sing with the understanding also." Notice, he did not say that God would take over and manipulate his mouth. He basically implied that this is a conscious choice of the will. After being filled with the Spirit, and having received access to the prayer language, we can use it at will.

When she asked us to sing in the Spirit, because I was at Gibeon and the guest speaker was at Zion, I couldn't receive the "new thing" God introduced through her. In actuality, it wasn't new to God. It was just new to me. It went against my tradition.

In Ephesians 4:11, we are shown the five-fold ministry God gave to the body of Christ; Apostles, Prophets, Evangelists, Pastors and Teachers.

Growing up in church, I didn't hear about that. We basically had the two-fold ministry; pastors and evangelists. The way you distinguished which office a person held was by determining how often they used their suitcases. Anyone who traveled on a regular basis was an evangelist. Oh, we had a few teachers. You always knew who they were. They had big charts which stretched from one side of the building to the other. (My apologies to those of you who did not grow up in this environment. This observation won't be nearly as funny for you as it is for me.)

The first time I heard someone referred to as a prophet, I thought, "What kind of a pompous egomaniac can this be?" I was "spitting out" the new thing.

I was fortunate enough to encounter someone who knows a lot more about Greek than I do. Fortunately, someone informed me that the original Greek word for "gave" in Ephesians 4:11 has a tense that we do not have in the English language. It basically means, "He did give, He does give, and will continue to give". I had always thought that the only apostles given to the church were given during the time that Jesus walked on earth. I now learned that He will continue to give all five ministries until, as it says in verse 13, "We all come into the unity of the faith". I don't think we've come into the unity of the faith yet. Obviously, He's still giving the five-fold ministry to the church.

God is doing new things on the earth today. I must admit that I am not comfortable with every new thing I experience. This may be because it doesn't fit with my tradition. It also may be, however, because it is not of God. Remember, just because something is old, it is not necessarily wrong. And just because something is new, that doesn't mean it's of God. We need everything that is authored by God, whether it is new or old. Just be sure you're where the glory is. If God is at Zion, what are you doing at Gibeon?

In Joshua chapter 3, we find the nation of Israel at the banks of the Jordan River, waiting to cross into the Promised Land. In verse 3, the people were told, "When ye see the Ark of the Covenant of the Lord your God, and the priests the Levites bearing it, then ye shall remove from your place, and go after it." In my opinion, this is God's plan for church growth. We spend so much of our time promoting programs and activities, we often forget the real issue -- it's all about the glory of God.

When people see the Ark--- God's glory, they will remove from their place and go after it. We need to ask ourselves, "Are people seeing the glory of God when they see us?"

When one alcoholic sees another, who was also once bound by alcohol, now set free by the glory of God, you won't have to beg him to come to church. He'll follow the glory. When the drug addict, the married couple on the verge of divorce, the person bound by depression, even the atheist or agnostic, see the glory of God, they will go after it. We need to focus our energies and attention on the restoration of God's glory. "Thy kingdom come ... on earth."

In 1980, on that first ministry trip to Australia, I had the privilege of speaking in some of the greatest churches in that nation. The man who invited me to the nation of Australia and organized that trip was Pastor David Cartledge, who pastored Calvary Temple in Townsville, a city in northern Queensland. I spent a week with them at Calvary Temple. What a great time in the Lord!

Remember, this trip to Australia was my introduction to "dancing before the Lord". As I was standing on the platform of Calvary Temple during the time of worship, many of the people had moved out of their seats, and were dancing in the front of the church, near the altar area. As I watched them, I focused on one of the young men, John Wedrat. As he danced before the Lord, I was drawn to his face. There was a look of adoration for God. I could see that he was dancing "to the right king".

While studying about God's glory, in 2 Corinthians 4:6, 1 found that God, "Who commanded the light to shine out of darkness, hath shined in our hearts, to give the light of the knowledge of the glory of God in the face of Jesus Christ." Verse 7 goes on to say that, "We have this treasure in earthen vessels, that the excellency of the power may be of God, and not of us." The face of Jesus Christ... God revealed His glory in Jesus' face.

What was it about Moses that was different when he came down from Mount Sinai after experiencing God's glory? It was his face. When Stephen was being stoned in Acts chapter 7, there was a young man by the name of Saul who held the coats of those stoning Stephen. Basically, he assisted in Stephen's slaughter. In today's terms he would be called an accessory to murder. While viewing the execution of this martyr, Saul became troubled by what he saw. Saul was so troubled that afterward, he went on a rampage, persecuting everyone who believed in "this Jesus whom Stephen preached". I believe that what he saw in Stephen "haunted" him until he surrendered, and accepted Jesus as his savior. Later he became the Apostle Paul, writing more than half of the New Testament.

What did he see? I believe it was the glory of God on Stephen's face. Eventually, he "removed from his place and went after it".

God is restoring the Tabernacle of David. As you and I make him king of our lives, Jesus' prayer is being answered. His kingdom is coming to earth, in us. Let His glory rest upon you. Let it shine through your face so others will "remove from their place and go after it".

"I just wanted to take a minute to thank you for your inspiration and spiritual guidance. My wife and I had the pleasure seeing you for the second time. We came away from that function with a better understanding of each other, a commitment to build a huge business, and on Sunday morning we both rededicated our lives to Jesus. You are the best, and we look forward to seeing and hearing you in the future."

S. P.

CHAPTER 8

THE THREE HEAVENS

Have you ever heard of the "Big Bang Theory"? Let me give you my version:

Thousands of years ago there was an explosion in the atmosphere. Out of this explosion came the sun, moon, and all of the planets in our solar system. The sun said, "I think I'll just sit here and rotate." The other planets said, "Rotation…that's a nice concept. We'll rotate too, but we want some variety in our lives. We'll keep moving in a circle around you. We'll call it 'orbiting.'" The sun agreed, so that's what they did.

On the earth, there was land and water. In the water were tiny microbe organisms, single-celled creatures floating in the sea. One of them began growing. More and more cells began developing. Eventually, it became hungry, so it grew a mouth. It needed to breathe, so it developed gills. It kept running into things, so it developed eyes. It couldn't move very fast, so it developed fins. (The better to swim with).

One day, this fish sighted land. It said, "I wonder what it's like to live up on the land." So, the gills closed up, the fins fell off, it grew four legs, and hopped up on the land. It was now a frog -- the first amphibian. One day the frog began climbing a tree and said, "In order to get to the next tree, I have to climb all the way back down, hop across the ground, and climb the next tree. Wouldn't it be great if I had longer arms and legs, hands with which to grip, and even a long tail? Then I could jump from tree to tree, mid-air." Boiiing!........The first monkey!

He really enjoyed playing in the trees, but one day he tried to jump too far. He fell to the ground. But when he fell, he landed on his feet. The hair fell out; his tail popped off. Surprise! The first man!

Now, if you had already studied the "Big Bang Theory", origin of species, or the theory of evolution, isn't my version more interesting? At least you could give it a "10" for entertainment value.

What amazes me is that some of the most ingenious minds in the world believe this rubbish! Doesn't that trouble you just a little? Why would someone so brilliant believe something so ridiculous? I believe it is because most scientists do not believe in anything they cannot measure...either by size, weight, volume, velocity, resistance, or some other physical reasoning. This is why they do not believe in the Creation story. They do not believe in the spiritual realm because it cannot be measured by physical means. Therefore, in order to find a cause for every effect they see around us, they must look within the physical realm. Thus, the ridiculous theories.

You and I know that there is a greater, mightier, more powerful realm than the physical realm. It is the spiritual realm. We also know that the origin of the sun, moon, stars, and our entire solar system is the spiritual realm. God spoke them into existence.

Hebrews 11:3 says, "Through faith we understand that the worlds were framed by the Word of God, so that things which are seen were not made of things which do appear." The original Greek for the words, "made of", actually mean "caused by". If we substitute those words, it would read like this, "...things which are seen were not caused by things which do appear."

If something is seen, is it seen in the physical or spiritual realm? Obviously, it would be the "physical". If something appears, in which realm would it appear? The answer again is "physical". Now, let us substitute this information into the text to help us understand it better: "...physical realm was not caused by physical realm." Do you agree? Of course, you do. We know that everything in the physical started in the spiritual. If we look deeply enough, we will find spiritual roots for every physical thing.

We believe this in regard to the creation story, but do we "live it out" in our daily lives?

Let's say you take your family on a picnic. It's a beautiful, bright, sunny day. A soft breeze is blowing in the trees. How wonderful to be alive! You set up the picnic table in the park. The food is taken from the picnic basket and arranged on the table in an inviting display. The family sits down together to begin the meal. Obviously, you pray over the food first. (Even pigs grunt before they eat.) You're enjoying your second bite of crispy fried chicken, when suddenly you hear a buzzing sound. You look up to see a radio-controlled airplane flying overhead. You say, "Look, kids, it's a remote-controlled airplane! Isn't that neat? I think it's flying in this direction. You can almost read the words on the side of the plane. Wow, it's really coming in close! Look out! Everyone under the table! It's coming at us!"

After assuring your family's safety under the picnic table, you crawl out on your hands and knees, grabbing a nearby baseball bat, and begin to chase the plane. You knock it out of the sky! You stomp on it…spit on it…in love! Then you say, "Now, that's over. We can get back to our meal."

About five minutes later, you hear that familiar buzzing sound again. You look up, in horror, to see another airplane headed straight at you. Hopefully, if you're not aclueistic, (Aclueistic is my own word. It means, "having no clue". Don't try to look this word up in the dictionary. If you do, it means that you are. If you would find it, it would say, "see mirror"). As I was saying, if you are not aclueistic, you will stop chasing airplanes and start looking for the guy with the remote control.

What we need to recognize is that behind every problem in our lives, there is a guy with a remote control. We are in the physical realm, and he is in the spiritual realm. We spend most of our lives chasing airplanes, and the guy with the remote control goes free. He has an inexhaustible resource of airplanes. You are not hurting him when you attack one. He will just pull another one out of the box and send it your way.

I am convinced that abortion of any type is murder. It's that simple. There are many Christians and Christian organizations who spend their whole lives addressing the physical aspect of abortion. (I realize that this is not true of everyone, but I do believe it to be true of many.) Because of my strong feelings against abortion, I will gladly sign your petitions, vote Pro-Life, and peaceably demonstrate with others who believe in the sanctity of human life. I do not, however, put all of my faith in these activities for the abolishment of abortion.

I do not believe that abortion was started by a greedy doctor who wanted to get rich by killing unborn children. Nor do I believe it was started by a selfish mother who found her unborn child to be an inconvenience. I am convinced that abortion was started by a demon...a guy with a remote control in the spiritual realm. His name is Murder. The abortionist and the mother are simply "airplanes" under his control. (Did you hear about the man who was going around killing abortion doctors a few years ago? When the authorities apprehended him and asked him why he had killed these people, he said it was because he was Pro-Life. This is a good time to use the word "aclueistic".)

Until we spend more time attacking the spiritual realm than we do the physical, we will never stomp out abortion.

As was stated previously, I am not opposed to doing what we can in the physical realm until the spiritual victory is realized. However, we should do so with the understanding that we will never win a victory through purely physical efforts. It is a spiritual battle.

In Ephesians 6 we are told of the "whole armor of God". Verse 12 says, "For we wrestle not against flesh and blood, but against principalities, against powers, against the rulers of the darkness of this world, against spiritual wickedness in high places." I am weary of hearing Christians say, "We wrestle not." There are those who construe this to mean that we do not wrestle. They are taking this completely out of context. In actuality, it states that we do wrestle; not against the physical realm, but against the spiritual realm. In fact, the Greek word for "high" in the phrase, "high places" is used eighteen times in the New Testament. In sixteen of those passages, it is more accurately translated "heaven" or "heavenly". In another passage, it is translated "celestial". Why is this the only case in which it is translated "high places"? We can only guess. Because this passage is speaking of evil and demonic activity, I wonder if the person who translated this in the early 1600's felt awkward speaking of demonic activity in "heavenly places".

Until God helped me to understand The Three Heavens, I had great difficulty with the concept of "spiritual wickedness in heavenly places."

Before we go further, it is necessary to mention the need for prac-
ticality in regard to spiritual matters. We are spiritual beings who
live in a physical world. I have encountered those who spiritualize
everything so much that they have lost the ability to be "real" in
their daily living. If you are walking down the street and you see a
man beating up a lady in a dark alley, don't run over to him and say:
"Now, sir, I can't touch you because I don't wrestle with flesh and
blood. I need to do spiritual warfare, so could you tell me exactly
what it is you are wanting to achieve. If you are simply wanting to
hurt her, then that would be a demon of violence. If you're wanting
to kill her, that would be a demon of murder. If you're wanting to
rob her, that would be a completely different category of demons."
By now, she's dead. Be practical! Knock him out! When he's lying
on the ground, you can lay hands on him, cast anything out of him,
or even anoint him with oil from head to foot. That's my definition
of practical Christianity.

In 2 Corinthians 10:2-4, Paul tells of a man who was caught up
to the "third heaven." He describes this place as "paradise" and says
in verse 4 (NIV) that while there, he heard "...inexpressible things,
things that man is not permitted to tell." This is obviously God's
heaven.

For years, I have heard people preach that paradise was a place
in the lower parts of the earth. Their sermons told us that is where
Jesus went after His death, to lead "captivity captive" and liberate
those who had been waiting in Abraham's bosom , who had died
"in the faith" before His death on the cross. Once, after teaching on
"The Three Heavens" in a church service, I was approached by some
people who had been taught the same thing. They wondered how
paradise could refer both to God's heaven and the "spiritual waiting
room" spoken of previously.

In answer, I told them that there is no place in the Bible, to my knowledge, in which that place (Abraham's bosom) was referred to as paradise. (That's a clue!) Also, by definition, paradise means, "the abode of God, the angels, and the righteous." Webster's dictionary calls it "a place of bliss." How could any of this apply to a place from which the Bible tells us Abraham and Lazarus could view those in hell in torment of flames?

If there is no reference to this place as paradise, why would anyone have called it that? I can only suppose that they based this on the words Jesus said to the thief on the cross next to Him, "Today shalt thou be with Me in paradise." Perhaps, because Jesus said they would be going to paradise, some assumed He was speaking of the first place He would visit before "...He ascended up on high". The place He visited in the "lower parts of the earth" was a brief stop, enroute to the final destination of God's heaven -- paradise -- the third heaven.

Suffice to say that the third heaven is the heaven where God is King.

Psalm 19:1 says, "The heavens declare the glory of God; and the firmament showeth His handiwork." This is a type of writing in which the second statement explains the first. We find it most commonly used in the book of Proverbs, in which a Proverb is set forth, and then followed by another Proverb which reinforces the principles stated in the previous one. Jesus also used this style of communication in the Lord's prayer, when He said, "Thy kingdom come, Thy will be done." As we mentioned previously, the latter statement explains the former.

With this understanding, we can see that the word "firmament" in the second statement is equated with the word "heavens" in the first. Basically, heavens and firmament in this passage are one and the same.

What is the firmament? It is the sky. Is the sun in the firmament? Yes. The moon? Yes. The earth? Yes. If so, then you and I are also in the firmament. The book you are holding is in the firmament. In fact, everything physical is in the firmament.

If scientists were to find a new solar system, millions of light-years from earth, would that also be in the firmament? Of course, it would. What I am saying is that as far as you can go in any direction, in the physical realm, you are in the firmament. The firmament is the physical realm and the physical realm is the firmament. As was previously stated, the firmament is a heaven. This is the first heaven.

Before we proceed further, let us first acknowledge that the book of Revelation is a book of prophecy. Most of the events detailed in that book have not yet occurred. The wars listed there have not yet been fought. In Revelation, when John speaks of things in the past tense, it is not because they have already occurred. It is because he is remembering in sequence what he saw in a vision, on the Isle of Patmos.

I am sure we would all agree that there will never be a war fought in God's heaven, the third heaven. This would relegate any wars to the first or second heavens. How would we know which one? If we look at those who are fighting the war, it will help to answer this question. If they are physical beings, they will fight in the physical realm, which is the first heaven. If, however, they are spiritual beings, they will fight in the spiritual realm...not in God's heaven, but in the second heaven.

Revelation 12: 7-8 (NIV) : "And there was war in heaven. Michael and his angels fought against the dragon, and the dragon and his angels fought back. But he was not strong enough, and they lost their place in heaven."

Since angels are spiritual beings, we know this war will be fought in the spiritual realm...the second heaven. Satan and his angels were cast out of God's heaven before Adam and Eve were created because of rebellion against God's authority. Because he is a spiritual being, satan could not come directly into the physical realm to establish his kingdom. He had to remain in the spiritual realm, but below God's heaven. Therefore, he is in the second heaven, between God and man. This is why we need spiritual warfare.

Many Christians believe that satan is in hell. He isn't. One day, he will be. But for now, he is the "prince of the power of the air."

Remember, there are three kings in this world; God, satan and self. If God is the king of the third heaven, and satan is king of the second heaven, who would be king of the first heaven? If you recall, we answered that question in our study on the glory of God. When God created man, He made him king in the physical realm. Three kings...three kingdoms...three heavens. That is why it is so important that we pray Jesus' prayer, "Thy kingdom come...on earth."

When we pray we stand in the physical realm, the first heaven. We pray to God in the spiritual realm, the third heaven. Every answer to prayer starts in the throne room of God, in the third heaven. To get to us in the first heaven, it must pass through the second heaven, where satan is king.

Everything we receive from God, we receive by faith. Picture your faith as an arm with a hand attached to the end of it. As you pray, your faith reaches through the first heaven, through the middle heaven into the presence of God. He places your answer in your hand of faith. You grip it tightly and begin pulling it back to yourself in the first heaven. As it approaches satan's territory in the second heaven, what do you think he does? Does he say, "All right, everyone out of the way. Answer to prayer coming through." Of course not! So what does he do?

Never forget this principle: Satan cannot take your answer to prayer out of your hand of faith. He doesn't have the power or the authority to do so. Never forget that.

Since he cannot take your answer to prayer away from you, he does the "next best thing". He delays it.

In Daniel, chapter 10, we read where Daniel had been praying for 21 days with seemingly no results. (Actually, I don't feel very sorry for him. I've waited a lot longer than 21 days for some answers to prayer! Have you?) An angel came to him in verse 10, informing him that, "...from the first day...thy words were heard". The delay had been caused by the "prince of the kingdom of Persia". The angel said that he "withstood me one and twenty days: but, lo, Michael, one of the chief princes, came to help me". The assistance in this battle had come from Michael, the Archangel of war.

Obviously, the word "prince" refers to an angel. The "prince of the kingdom of Persia" is a fallen angel...a demon. We refer to him as a territorial demon. He has been assigned to Persia, which is modern-day Iran, Iraq and Kuwait. Do you think he's still around? What was the name of the gulf where the war took place in between Kuwait and Iraq? Do you remember where we sent our troops? It is called the Persian Gulf. The prince of Persia is alive and well today. The same territorial demon who hindered Daniel's prayer is still causing trouble today.

In the seventies, we thought Ayatollah Khomeini was the problem. When he died, we assumed the trouble in Persia was over. Then, in the eighties, along comes Saddam Hussein. When he is gone, there will be another. They are just remote-controlled airplanes, and the prince of Persia is the guy with the remote control. Until he is defeated, Persia will not have peace.

Can you think of a few other territorial demons? Do you think there might be one over New York, Miami, Chicago, my home city of New Orleans, Los Angeles, San Francisco, your city? What about other nations? When we think in spiritual terms we can see that the pain, oppression and devastation in these places is not merely the result of the selfishness of man. It starts in the spiritual realm, and until we defeat the guys with the remote controls, there will be no peace or victory.

This is why I tell people that they need to attack the spiritual root of a problem, rather than to use only the "weed-eater", which deals only with the "visible" things in the physical realm. If your brother-in-law is bound by alcoholism, he will not quit drinking just because you beat him up. Admittedly, it may make you feel better to pound your fist with his face, but it won't solve the problem. The problem is not a bottle of alcohol. It is a guy with a remote control. There is a demon of alcoholism who is influencing him. Until that demonic influence is broken over his life, he can never be free.

That is why Jesus could look at Peter and bind the devil. In His wisdom he recognized that, although Peter had been wrong in what he said, the true source of the problem was satan. Jesus was angry with Peter, but He attacked satan.

If you know someone who is bound in a false religion or cult, please don't argue with them. I've heard Christians brag about their arguments with members of cults: "I work with this guy who is in a cult, and yesterday he and I had a long argument. I made him look so stupid, praise God!" In the Great Commission, Jesus did not say, "Go ye into all the world and make people look stupid." The only one who wins an argument is the devil. He has successfully brought division. Even if that person eventually realizes that you were right, do you honestly believe that he will come running to you and say, "You were right. I was wrong. I can't believe how stupid I was!" The best thing to do in these situations is to share truth with them, as long as they are open. If you sense that they are becoming defensive, "drop it" and go to prayer in their behalf when they are not around. This is called "covert warfare".

People who are bound in a cult have welcomed the influence of a demonic prince in their life. He now distorts everything they hear and see. Suddenly, truth looks like a lie, and lies appear to be true. It is like a "fun-house mirror" at the county fair. Everything is distorted.

If you tell the person truth, what does he think you are doing? He is convinced that you are lying. Until this demonic influence is broken, he will not hear or see the truth for what it is. You should first spend time in prayer, in order to identify the demon who has sway over him.

Remember, when you are binding him, the individual may still be welcoming his influence into his life. In effect, you tie him up and they loosen the knots. That is why we must "pray without ceasing". When the demon's influence is broken, you will then be able to speak truth into his life and have him hear it as truth.

There was a young lady in my dad's church in New Orleans who heard me teach on this. Her sister was caught up in a cult. The Christian lady used these principles in regard to her sister. She made her sister a dress and prayed over every stitch. She did warfare against the deceiving spirit. Within a short period of time, her sister accepted Jesus and was set free from this deception.

Let us get back to your answer to prayer. Remember, it is still in the middle heaven. When we left off, satan had delayed it there. He can not take it away from you...only delay it. While the answer is held up, satan causes things to happen in the physical realm in order to make you believe that the prayer will never be answered. Remember, everything in the physical starts in the spiritual. Because satan is in the spiritual realm, he makes things happen in the physical sphere, which have nothing to do with the actual status of your answer to prayer.

You are praying for a family member's salvation. Instead of them getting saved, they get worse. You are praying for a healing in your body. Instead of receiving healing, you start hurting in a new spot. You are praying for a financial breakthrough, and you receive a new bill you didn't even know you owed. What is happening? Satan is at it again. He is trying to get us to take our progress report from the physical realm instead of the spiritual realm. The real battle is in the spiritual realm.

God came to Abraham and asked him if he would like to have a child -- a little boy to bounce on his knee, someone to carry on his family name. Abraham was thrilled. He was told of Isaac by faith. Isaac was not yet in the physical realm. He still existed only in the spiritual one. I can relate to Abraham much better than Daniel, because he had to wait 25 years!

Satan delayed Isaac's birth in the middle heaven. Meanwhile, Abraham and Sarah were looking for progress reports in the physical realm. When nothing happened, they decided to "help God". What a foolish move! In order to "make things happen" in the physical realm, they released what was in their hand in the spiritual. They let go of Isaac!

Satan cannot take our answer to prayer from our hand of faith. If we fall for his deception, however, we will "let go" of what was once ours. When this happens, he grabs it up and stores it in his kingdom. Poor little Isaac was floating in the middle heaven for all those years!

I have people ask me, "If I have let go of an answer to prayer, can I ever get it back?" Did Abraham and Sarah get Isaac back? The key is to recognize our error and go back to working in the spiritual realm instead of the physical.

Jesus said in Matthew 12:29, "...how can one enter into a strong man's house, and spoil his goods, except he first bind the strong man? And then he will spoil his house." Is Jesus teaching us how to steal? Obviously not! Then why is He telling us how to take something from someone else? Because it is ours. It is stolen property. It belongs to us.

He warns us that, before retrieving what is ours, we must first bind (tie up) the one who stole from us -- who holds our property. Only after the demon is incapacitated may we safely recover what is ours. I have seen many Christians, myself included, come under attack while attempting to redeem stolen belongings. The problem was that we did not bind the strongman before entering his house. Understand, this is war. Satan plays for keeps. You must play by the rules, or you get hurt.

Can you think of something you let go? Perhaps you were thrown off by what you saw happening in the physical realm, and you simply gave up the hope of that prayer ever being answered. Isn't it time to reclaim what is yours? How would you feel about marching into the devil's territory and returning home with an answer to prayer in your hands?

One of my favorite Bible characters is the prophet Elisha. There was a time when God revealed to him that the Syrian army was setting a trap for the Israelites. Elisha told the king, and the king warned the Israeli army in time to avoid defeat. Time and again, God warned Elisha with specific information regarding the Syrian army. The king of Syria became frustrated because it seemed that he would never be able to defeat the Israelites. He called together all of his captains and inquired as to whether any of them had revealed their troop movements to the Israelis. They said, "No, King, none of us." He then asked if they had any idea who it could be. They told him of the prophet Elisha. When they learned where he lived, the Syrian army surrounded the city where Elisha lived. The next morning, as his servant, Gehazi, saw the armies, he ran to Elisha in a state of panic. Elisha said, "What is it?" Gehazi replied, "Oh, it is just terrible!"

"What is?"

"Oh, I can't even say! It is just horrible!"

"Oh, I'd must go and look for myself."

When Elisha looked out, he said, "Glory to God! This is fantastic!"

Gehazi asked, "In which direction were you looking?"

Then Elisha prayed, "Father, open his eyes that he may see."

He reminded Gehazi that, they who are with us are more than they who are against us. When Gehazi looked again he saw that between him and the Syrian army, was a mightier, more powerful army than the Syrians. It was an army of angels! Suddenly, faith rose in him to believe for victory.

Where was the army of angels the first time Gehazi looked out? They were there. He just didn't see them. He was taking his progress report from the physical realm, and they were in the spiritual realm.

You may ask, "Well, if the angels were there, whether or not he saw them, it wouldn't make a difference. They would still defend him." I don't think so. The Bible says, "As your faith is, so be it unto you." I am convinced that the armies of the Lord are frequently surrounding His children, prepared to protect us. Because of our lack of spiritual perception and because we take our progress from the physical realm; we don't appropriate faith for the victory. Therefore, we are defeated.

My prayer for you today is that God will "open your eyes, so that you may see that they who are with you are more than they who are against you." I also pray that you would take your progress report from the spiritual realm and not the physical.

After God gave me understanding about the three heavens, it answered some of the questions I once had about certain passages in the Bible. One of those is found in Matthew 16:19 and again in Matthew 18:18. It states that whatever we bind on earth will be bound in heaven, and whatever we loose on earth will be loosed in heaven. When I thought in terms of only one heaven, I could not understand binding (tying up) anyone or anything in God's heaven. Why would I want to bind angels, or even God? And was there anything in God's heaven which was tied up and needed to be loosed?

Once I understood that there are three heavens, I then saw with greater clarity. Although I do not wish to bind anything or anyone in the third heaven, there are some guys with remote controls in the middle heaven who definitely need to be tied up. I also understood that my stolen property in satan's heaven needs to be loosed. As Jesus taught us: bind, then loose.

Another passage with which I had difficulty was Malachi 3:10, where God says that if we will tithe, He will open the "windows of heaven" to pour out blessings upon us. I wondered why God had installed windows in His heaven, which could withhold blessings from us. In Psalm 84:11, it says, "...no good thing will He withhold from them that walk uprightly."

After coming to an understanding of the three heavens, I then realized that the windows are not on God's heaven. I believe they are on satan's heaven, the middle heaven. When we submit ourselves to God through tithing, God "moves heaven" (satan's heaven) to bless us.

In closing, let me remind you that things which are seen are not caused by things which do appear. Isaiah 53:1 says, "Who hath believed our report? And to whom is the arm of the Lord revealed?"

To hear God's report...to see His strong arm, we must be spiritually minded. He is on our side.

"You've become a hero to me a few times now. Your intellect is absolutely inspirational. I do believe anyone who has had the blessing to have heard you in the course of his/her life is invariably called to a higher standard. You make a difference, Mark. You duplicate yourself in others because you say so much in love. I will always thank God for at least having given me the opportunity to hear you."
L. S. FROM WISCONSIN

CHAPTER 9

THE WEAPON OF PRAISE

Matthew 11:12 was another of those verses with which I had struggled for understanding. In this passage, Jesus says that, "...the kingdom of heaven suffereth violence, and the violent taketh by force." As you can see, I am a very logical person. Things have to make sense. In this passage, it appears that Jesus is encouraging us to be violent with heaven. In my mind I asked, "Why would Jesus encourage me to be violent with God?"

Once I understood the three heavens, I realized that there is one heaven which only understands violence, and only the violent will take that heaven by force. I do not believe Jesus was referring to God's heaven, the third heaven. I am of the opinion that He was speaking of the second heaven.

This also applies, I believe, to what He said in Matthew 16:19, when He said that He would give us the keys to the kingdom of heaven. I do not believe there are any locks to keep the Christian out of the presence of God in the third heaven. I believe Jesus was telling us that with the power to bind and loose, we have the "keys" to lock and unlock in satan's domain, the middle heaven.

When Jesus taught us to pray, He began His prayer with these words, "Our Father which art in heaven, hallowed be Thy name." First, we establish relationship...Our Father. Secondly, we acknowledge His authority...which art in heaven. Thirdly, we offer praise and worship. It is interesting to note that the first three requests in the Lord's Prayer were on behalf of God; hallowed be Thy name, Thy kingdom come, Thy will be done. Is this how we pray?

To be successful in prayer, we must learn the effective use of one of the greatest weapons in the Christian arsenal. That is the weapon of praise.

It seems to me that before lucifer was banished from God's heaven, there were three archangels. One was in charge of warfare and all warring angels. His name is Michael. Another was in charge of communication, and ministering angels. His name is Gabriel. The third was in charge of praise, worship, music and dance. His name is lucifer.

I have seen some Christians who, because of revelation God has given them regarding praise and worship, have become lifted up in pride, and considered themselves superior to other Christians because of their new-found freedom in worship. Just keep in mind, lucifer was worshipping, harboring a similar attitude of pride, when he was banished from God's presence.

It seems that God did not express the desire to create man until lucifer and all of the praising angels were expelled from the third heaven. God created us for fellowship, praise, and worship. Do you ever wonder why satan hates you so much? You got his job! Every time we praise God, we remind satan that he was fired, and we are the replacements.

Sometimes, I think God has a neat sense of humor. Of all the possibilities He could have chosen for use as a weapon, He chose the very thing that satan once did. When we praise the Lord, not only do we remind satan that we got his job, we also remind him that he no longer works for the King of Kings and Lord of Lords. Praise drives back satan's forces.

Before we go further into this study, we must look at the three heavens a bit more closely. As we gain more understanding about them, it will enable us to better understand the role of praise in spiritual warfare.

Because the first heaven is the entire physical realm, we know that it is here, where we are. That's a given!

Now, do we believe that there are angels and demons around us? Yes, we obviously do. Because of this, we know that the spiritual realm is also here. You may ask, "How can the spiritual realm and the physical realm be at the same place?" The answer is that the spiritual does not take up physical space. When Jesus came into your heart, you didn't swell up! Can you imagine going to a tailor and saying, "I need you to let out my clothing. I asked Jesus into my heart, and I swelled up. But you'd better let them out all the way. I'm seeking to be filled with the Holy Ghost!"

Spiritual beings do not take up physical space. Therefore, the spiritual and physical realms can co-exist.

If demons and angels are around us, we know that the second heaven is here as well. (Remember, there are three heavens. Everything exists in one of those three.) Understand, we are not limiting the size or dimensions of any of the three heavens. We are merely acknowledging the co-existence of spiritual and physical in the same place.

Now let us tackle the "biggie". You are probably worried that I'll try to take away your trip. Don't get nervous. I believe that when the Bible says we shall be caught up to meet the Lord in the air, which means we will literally be transported to another place.

Let us look at this objectively. In the Bible we are told of a heavenly city. We have assumed that to be the entirety of God's heaven. If so, why is it called a "city"? My city, New Orleans, is an American city, but I cannot say that New Orleans is America. The term "city" denotes a portion of a larger territory.

Were you to ask some Christians where the devil is, they would say, "He's everywhere, he's everywhere." Yet, if asked where God is, they would say, "He's far, far away, in a city built foursquare." Why do we relegate God to the city limits of that heavenly city and think of satan as being omnipresent?

What is it that makes heaven? If I were to pave the street in front of your home with gold, would that make it heaven? If we put walls of jasper and gates of pearl around the city where you live, and built mansions throughout, would that make it heaven? No.

Well, we're told that heaven has streets of gold, gates of pearl, walls of jasper, etc. If those things would not make your city heaven, what does make heaven, heaven? It is the presence of God...His glory. God makes heaven, heaven.

If that is true, what does He make of your heart when He comes there?

In my opinion, heaven is not limited to that city built foursquare. That is but a part, a small portion of God's heaven. I believe that heaven is wherever God is. He makes it heaven. I have been in church services when the glory of God would fall on the place, and someone leading the service would say, "I believe we're experiencing a little bit of heaven right here on earth." I think that is accurate.

Because God's kingdom (the third heaven), and satan's kingdom (the second heaven) are both in the spiritual realm, they cannot co-exist. When God's kingdom is established, satan's kingdom is displaced by it.

Have you ever been praying when you felt that your prayers just weren't getting through? You wondered if God even heard what you were saying. My dad says that we can pray for two hours and wonder if God heard us...and yet, we hit our finger with a hammer and say one curse word and we know God heard it. We are not sure if He heard that two hours of prayer, but we know He heard that one curse word. Isn't that ridiculous?

God always hears our prayers. As I stated previously, He even knows what we are going to pray before we say it. When we feel that our prayers are not getting through, I believe it is actually the presence of satanic forces, oppressing us. At that moment, we are surrounded by the second heaven, by satan's armies. That means it's time for war!

When Israel went into battle, there was one tribe that always went first. As you know, that was the tribe of Judah. One of the meanings of the name of Judah means "praise". Symbolically, God was teaching us, as Jesus taught us in the Lord's prayer, which we should always approach warfare with praise going before us.

Interestingly, Strong's Concordance lists one of the root words for Judah as "Yadah". I was thrilled as I read some of the meanings for that word: "to throw (a stone, an arrow) ...to revere or worship (with extended hands)...praise, shoot". Isn't it amazing that the same word speaks of reverence and worship for God, while also speaking of throwing stones and arrows and shooting? To me, this makes it obvious that praise is a formidable weapon against satan.

When you feel surrounded by a demonic presence, the most strategic thing you can do is to lift up your hands and praise the Name of the Lord. Your praises bombard the middle heaven. When you say, "Thank you, Jesus. I love you Lord. I praise Your Name", you are "throwing stones and arrows" at the demons around you, and "shooting" at the forces of the enemy. Now that's warfare.

When Paul and Silas were thrown into prison, they found themselves surrounded by evil and wickedness. As you know, demons congregate where they feel most comfortable. Can you imagine the depression, anger, and violence in that place? In those days, they did not have the convenience of modern plumbing facilities. The stench and the filth in that place would have turned your stomach.

Paul turned to Silas and said, "If we make bail and get out of here tonight, I'm gonna praise the Lord." Ha! No, he didn't! But how many of us would say that? All too often, we wait for God to move, so we can praise Him for what He has done. We need to understand that you thank Him for what He has done. You praise Him for what He is able to do. God is worthy of praise whether things are going the way we want them to or not. Regardless of my circumstances, He is worthy. If you are waiting for God to get you out of prison, out of those marital problems, that physical problem, your financial crisis before you praise Him, you had better get comfortable. You may to be there for a while.

Paul and Silas understood the function of praise. The circumstances had not changed. Things looked as bleak now as they did five minutes ago. The situation was hopeless. But they praised God anyway. God was worthy of their praise, regardless of their circumstances.

As they began to lift up the Name of the Lord, throwing those stones and arrows into the middle heaven, demons began to shrink back in horror. "They're shooting at us! Run for it!"

Suddenly the atmosphere began to change in that darkened prison cell. The Kingdom of God began to displace the kingdom of satan. The glory of God, the third heaven filled that place with such intensity that the substructure of the building was incapable of handling its awesome power. The walls began to shake, the doors to the prison cells swung open, and they were set free. And just to think, it all started with praise.

Why does God inhabit the praise of His people? Because, as our praises break through satan's territory and drive back his demonic forces, the glory of God, His presence, rains down upon us and fills the "habitation" we have made with our praises. Ephesians 2:6 says that God has "...raised us up together, and made us sit together in heavenly places in Christ Jesus." How can we sit in heavenly places? Either God has some serious highchairs or, perhaps, instead of moving us to His heaven, our praises move heaven to us.

In Acts, chapter 7, Stephen was martyred for the cause of Christ. As the stones were being hurled at his body, breaking bones and crushing vital organs, the life was draining from him. Instead of becoming bitter, or feeling sorry for himself, he continued to lift up the Name of the Lord. Suddenly, he said, "Behold, I see, far, far away, a little bitty city with a little, bitty throne and a little, bitty God and a tiny little Jesus." Is that what he said? Absolutely not!

In Acts 7:56, he said, "Behold, I see the heavens opened, and the Son of Man standing on the right hand of God." The first heaven had been pushed back. The second heaven had been displaced, and he was standing face to face with the throne of God, directly before Him. God was not far off viewing his death from some remote location. God's presence, the third heaven, was right in front of him.

In the midst of our greatest trials, we can experience the presence of God by simply doing that for which we were created: praising His name.

Let us not forget that before Jesus ascended into heaven, He told us in John 14:2, that He was going to prepare a place for us. His purpose for telling us of the beauty of that heavenly city was to inspire us to persevere and keep pressing on. Believe me, just one moment on those streets of gold will make it worth any sacrifice we have made here on earth. Until then, just keep praising Him.

My husband and I have recently been introduced to your ministry through my husband's brother. I began reading The Three Heavens and with every page I felt more and more blessed. Please thank Mark for what he is doing and let him know that we absolutely love him and his style.

L.Z. FROM CALIFORNIA

CHAPTER 10

THE SWORD OF THE SPIRIT

Ephesians 6:14-17, "Stand therefore, having your loins girt about with truth, and having on the breastplate of righteousness; and your feet shod with the preparation of the gospel of peace; above all, taking the shield of faith, wherewith ye shall be able to quench all the fiery darts of the wicked. And take the helmet of salvation, and the sword of the Spirit, which is the Word of God:"

In this passage, Paul lists six different articles in the "whole armor of God". Note that five of the six are for defense. Only one is to be used for attacking the enemy in battle. Using this ratio as a guide, I suggest that before engaging in warfare, one should expend five times the effort, energy and time in preparing for battle, as you will spend engaged in battle.

In this chapter we will deal with the latter of the six weapons, the sword of the Spirit – the only "offensive" weapon mentioned in

Ephesians 6.

The two main Greek words used in the New Testament for "word" are "logos" and "rhema". Basically, "logos" speaks of a written word and "rhema" speaks of a spoken word.

The way I see it, when someone speaks a word to you, it is a "rhema". When you write down what they have said, it becomes a "logos". The entire Bible was "rhema" when God spoke it to those who wrote it down. It was "rhema" in their hearts, as they heard God speak it, and became "logos" when they transferred it to parchment. Because of this, the entire Bible is "logos". It only becomes "rhema" when it is spoken.

In verse 17 of Ephesians 6, in regard to the sword of the Spirit, we are told that it is the "rhema" of God. Notice that is specifically says, "rhema of God". It is important for us to understand this. It means that I cannot, at will, select a verse and use it as a sword in warfare. You may say, "But if I speak it, it will become a "rhema".

Look more closely at the verse. Your name is not listed in the verse. It must be a rhema of God, not a rhema of Mark or Sue or Bill. Therefore, God must be speaking that word through you as you do battle.

I feel that there has been an error in some of the teaching regarding speaking the word. Some who have heard the word of faith taught, have moved from faith into presumption, by assuming that whatever they speak is the rhema of God.

If you were to go into a court of law, and testify that you know for a fact that the defendant committed the crime. You based this on the fact that your hairdresser's cousin has a plumber whose mother-in-law went on a cruise and met a lady whose nephew is the chiropractor for the defendant's dentist. You heard from this accurate source that the defendant, while in the dentist's chair, under the influence of Nitrous Oxide (laughing gas), readily admitted to the crime. Would you be shocked if they did not admit your testimony as evidence? By a slight technicality, your testimony would be ruled as "hearsay".

When we come to satan, speaking God's word, if God's Spirit is not simultaneously speaking it through us, satan dismisses it as hearsay, because it is not the spoken Word of God. It is the spoken word of Mark or Sue or Bill. Remember, the seven sons of Sceva tried this, and it didn't work for them. (Acts, chapter 19)

Before I speak something as rhema, it must become rhema to me. By this I mean that I must experience God's Spirit speaking His Word into my spirit, in order for it to be a rhema of God in my life.

In my opinion, no one has received rhema from God for every verse in the Bible. That is why we benefit from hearing different men and women of God, as they speak forth what God has revealed to them, as rhema.

Romans 10:17 says that faith comes by hearing, and that hearing comes by the "Word of God". Once again, because I am so logic-oriented, I had to make sense of this. How could God's word bring hearing? That's what it was saying. Someone told me, "That means the Bible on tape." Well, I knew that couldn't be true because it wouldn't be fair to those born before Alexander Scourby. (He's the first man to record the entire Bible.)

But what did Romans 10:17 mean? It said that hearing comes by God's Word. Once again I asked, "How can God's Word bring hearing?"

One day as I was praying, God helped me to understand this. After all, He's the One who wrote it. He should know what it means. He said that this is not speaking of hearing with the natural ear.

Think about it. Is faith in the physical or spiritual realm? It is spiritual. Therefore, faith is in my spirit...not in my mind. Hearing someone speak God's Word to my mind does not bring faith. God's Word only becomes faith when it "connects" with my spirit. How can a man, who is physical, speak to my spirit? He cannot. Therefore, the only one who can speak to my spirit is another spirit. As I sit in a church service, listening to someone preach, they are communicating with my intellect and emotions. If, while they are speaking, God's Spirit rests upon them, He takes what they are saying in the natural, and speaks it into my spirit. There is an explosion of growth in my faith when this happens. Faith is birthed in me, as the rhema of God, spoken by His Spirit, germinates within me.

After receiving a rhema from God, it remains rhema in me. It is as though God perpetually speaks that word into my spirit again and again, keeping it fresh and building my faith. Now when I speak that word, if I am anointed by God's Spirit, and flowing in His Spirit, it remains a rhema of God when it comes forth...not because I am speaking it, but because He is speaking it through me as I say it.

Have you ever been reading your Bible when a verse suddenly seemed to jump off the page? (If this hasn't happened to you, perhaps you should read your Bible more.) When God emphasizes a scripture in this way, He is trying to tell you something. The worst thing you could do is to keep reading. Stop! Back up, read it again, close your eyes and meditate on it. Let God's Spirit speak it into your spirit, as a rhema of God. He will reveal it to you in such a way that it becomes faith within you. Now, you can use it in your arsenal for warfare.

At this point, it would be good for us to focus on the purpose of the sword. It is designed for attacking an enemy and delivering a fatal blow. Let us keep in mind who the enemy is. I have seen Christians use the Word of God as a weapon on sinners, practically destroying them with the voracity of their scriptural argument. God's Word is to be a seed for the sinner. God never said it should be planted with a shotgun. Sometimes we could achieve much more by talking to God than when we talk to the sinner. Personal witnessing must be coupled with a Spirit-led life, if it is to be effective.

In other circumstances, I have observed as Christians use the Word as a sword on their brothers and sisters in Christ. Christians are not our enemies. We're in the same army. The Word should be used as a scalpel to bring surgical healing in a Christian. Ephesians 4:15 admonishes us to speak "the truth in love". The word of God you speak into the life of a brother or sister in Christ may be truth, but is it being spoken in love? What is your motive? What are you seeking as an end result, healing or destruction?

We have eliminated two of our favorite uses for the sword. Since we can't use it to attack Christians or sinners, what else can we do with it? As a last resort, let's use it on satan.

Several years ago, a friend of our family was in New Orleans attending a Christian Oilmen's Convention. (By the way, that reminds me of something I heard about which happened during the last oil crisis in Texas). Two ladies, I am told, were walking down a street in Houston. Suddenly they heard a voice saying, "Ladies!" They turned to find a frog on the sidewalk. "If one of you will kiss me", he explained, "I'll turn into a Texas oil tycoon." One of the ladies hurriedly picked up the frog and placed him in her purse. The other enquired, "Why didn't you kiss him?" "Are you crazy?" she replied. "A talking frog is worth a lot more than a Texas oil tycoon!"

Where was I? Oh, yes, the Christian Oilmen's Convention in New Orleans. One of the conference speakers was a Spirit-filled Catholic priest, who was director of an orphanage in a small Texas town, near the Mexican border. He was somewhat frail looking, in his traditional black shirt and clerical collar, with black jeans and black tennis shoes. He was carrying a large Catholic Bible, which appeared to be at least half as big as he was. I wondered, "What is this little guy going to say to change my life?" Boy, did he blow my mind!

He started by saying, "I want to talk to you about speaking the Word." Immediately I thought, "Could you have chosen a topic that has been used more? I don't think so." Now, I'm ashamed of what I thought. God used that man to speak into my life.

He said that God had taught them how to speak the Word into the spiritual realm, as a command to satan and his demons. He said, "We never take it upon ourselves to choose which passage we should use in a given situation. Before speaking the Word, we spend much time in prayer, asking God to reveal to us the Word that He wants to accomplish in that situation." (Sounds like a rhema to me.)

He told several stories of miracles which happened as a result of them speaking the Word. Let me share a couple of those with you.

They had been invited to minister in a prison for young men in Mexico. Many other ministries had come there previously, only to leave disheartened because of the terrible response from the prisoners. They would scream and shout profanity so loudly that the ministry could not be heard. The prison officials had decided to not allow anyone else to come into the prison for ministry, but acquiesced to allow this one group for a "final try".

While praying, God gave them Philippians 2:10-11, "That at the name of Jesus every knee should bow...And that every tongue should confess that Jesus Christ is Lord, to the glory of God the Father."

The priest explained that they actually do three different things; one third of the group speaks that Word, another third prays in tongues, and the others sing, praise and dance before the Lord.

The prison buildings were configured in a "U" shape, with a courtyard area in the middle. The young men in the prison were so violent that the officials decided to not remove them from their cells. They would have to look through the bars on the windows of their cells and carefully listen to observe and hear the ministry in the courtyard below. The ministry group, led by this Spirit-filled Catholic priest, set up their sound equipment in the central courtyard and began to minister in song. He said that the screaming and shouting of profanity was so loud they could not hear the music coming through the sound system. That's loud!

He turned to the group and told one third of them to continue singing, praising, and dancing before the Lord. He then told others to pray in the spirit, and a third group to begin speaking the rhema word God had given them for that occasion. They began saying, "At the name of Jesus, every knee shall bow. At the name of Jesus, every knee shall bow."

After 30 minutes (that's a long time), no change. They kept speaking the word, praying in the Spirit and praising the Lord.

After one hour, still no change. Some of the group was beginning to lose their voices. They had to stagger the singing and speaking, while others rested their voices.

An hour-and-a-half had gone by and the prisoners continued to shout their profanities. I don't know about you, but I would have had a tendency to "shake the dust off my feet" and go home. The priest explained that God had told them to not stop speaking the Word that He had given them until it came to pass.

So........they kept speaking the Word, "At the name of Jesus, every knee shall bow." They didn't give up. Isaiah 55:11 says, "So shall my word be that goeth forth out of my mouth: It shall not return unto me void, but it shall accomplish that which I please, and it shall prosper in the thing whereto I sent it."

Finally, after one hour and forty-five minutes, every prisoner was on his knees. "At the name of Jesus, every knee shall bow."

When God gives you a rhema, keep speaking it until the principalities obey and come in line with the Word of God.

Romans 4:17 says that God "calleth those things that be not as though they were." Regardless of what you see around you, remember, everything in the physical starts in the spiritual. Through eyes of faith, see what God has ordained for your life. Speak the word He has spoken to you, command it into the heavenlies. It becomes a sword in the hands of the Christian warrior.

On another occasion, the priest said that several of the young people were coming to him and expressing concern about their friends in public school. They said, "They are going to these rock concerts and getting involved in drugs and sex. What can we do for them?" They agreed to spend time in prayer, asking God for the verses He would have them to use (rhema). After a season of prayer, God gave them a collection of verses which they called their "rock bomb".

They sought out information regarding the concert arena used by the rock bands who held concerts in a nearby city. It just "so happened" that on the same property with the arena was another, smaller building. They rented the smaller facility under the name of an individual, not the orphanage (covert warfare).

On the day of the next concert, they gathered in the rented building to do warfare. Approximately two hours before each concert, they began their time of prayer, praising God and speaking the Word.

On the day following each concert, the young people from the orphanage would ask their schoolmates whether or not they had enjoyed the concert. He said that some of the results were more subtle than others. Sometimes, they would just say, "Oh, it wasn't all that great." At other times, the results were much more obvious, such as, "You wouldn't believe it! In the middle of the second song, the lead singer lost his voice and they had to close the concert."

One of the concert tours had to be canceled, forfeiting the next six weeks of concert dates, because the lead singer lost his voice in their city.

On one occasion, as they were praying in the rented building, the prophets told the priest that they were doing some "serious damage in the spiritual realm". He looked outside and noticed that no one had entered the auditorium. Walking over to some of the young concert-goers, he inquired as to why they had not yet entered the coliseum. He noted that the concert should have started already. They said, "Oh, no one can go into the auditorium yet. They are having trouble with the sound system. They can't get it to work. What they do not understand is that the electrical outlets in the building have been tested and they are fine, but the sound equipment won't turn on."

He hurriedly went back into the building to give this progress report to the rest of the group. They rejoiced together, then continued with their three-fold warfare activity for about 30 more minutes, and went home rejoicing in their victory. About 30 minutes after they left the property, the sound system started working again.

After the concert, no other rock groups would come into that city.

He said that word got out among the rock bands that there was a "jinx" on that arena.

My suggestion to you is that you learn, as I did, from this Spirit-filled Catholic priest. I believe this is God's plan for the use of His Word as a sword. Remember, when God gives you a "rhema", keep speaking it until it comes to pass.

I just love your book The 3 Heavens. Never have I seen such an in depth, easily read, concise book on spiritual warfare as yours. After reading the book, I realize that the years of focusing on my circumstances have caused me to give up on my hopes and dreams. You have given me the faith to reach out and reclaim what God has already promised me.

G. C. FROM TENNESSEE

CHAPTER 11

Practical Principles For Warfare

How do I know if I have on the "whole armor of God"? James says that God's word is like a mirror, which shows me what "manner of man" I am. Everything God speaks to us, He does by using the Word and the Spirit. Without the Spirit, the Word lacks life. Without the Word, the operation of the Spirit may lack balance.

As God's Spirit reveals His word to me, it can be used to reveal areas in my life where I am missing armor, where I do not "line up" with the Word.

Many Christians feel a false sense of security because, as far as they know, their lives agree with the Word. Unfortunately, however, they are getting dressed, using a bathroom cabinet mirror, not a full-length mirror. By this I mean that they are not allowing the entire Word of God to speak into their lives. They have their favorite topics and favorite verses, and only want to receive from the Word if it has to do with that subject.

Some say while flitting about, "I just want to hear about love. If it's about holiness or anything that brings conviction, I'm not interested. I like to hear that God loves me and giggles when I sin."

Others say, with their teeth tightly clenched, "I want to hear about righteousness, holiness, and clean livin'. I like it 'cause it makes me smile. Don't go easy on 'em. Make 'em smell the smoke from the flames of hell."

Still others will say with a faraway look in their eyes, "I just want to hear about prophecy. Do you have a word for me? I just love it when I get a word. How about this? You give me a word, and then I'll give you a word. By the way, could I get a word for my mother?"

And there are still others who I call "warfare groupies". They say, "I just want to shoot somethin'. I'm a militant for Jesus. Let's bust up some demons. Make 'em hurt. Let's shoot somethin'."

In each of these extremes, there is truth. Unfortunately, the truth of God's Word has been skewed and distorted by excess. You see, when we specialize on one subject, we usually end up running out of material on which to teach. Then we must start making it up, just to keep our following.

If you hear much of my teaching, you will hear a recurring word; "balance". It concerns me when I see people who take one principle from the Word of God and run so far and so fast with it, that they go beyond the parameters of God's Word. This is what I mean by the term "medicine cabinet mirror". By looking at the portion of God's Word with which they agree, they feel secure, it appears that they have on the "whole armor of God." In reality they may only be clothed from the waist up, because that is all they can see.

In an effort to bring some balance to the warfare teachings which are circulating today, and at the risk of offending some of those who espouse them, I feel that I must share from my heart.

We are all familiar with 2 Chronicles 7:14, in which God tells us that He will heal our land, if we meet certain criteria. Few verses have been quoted or preached from as often as this passage. The mistake made by so many of us is that we have missed the first three words of the verse, "If My people..."

Like many of you, I have derived a certain joy from listening to extremely conservative radio and television commentators, who summarily dismiss our nation's leaders as the villains who are to blame for the present condition of America. I have found that, although I agree with many of their political views, when I listen to them too often, I begin to take on that critical spirit and find it easy to criticize our leaders, placing the blame completely on them. We need to be reminded of Paul's words in Acts 23:5(NIV), "Do not speak evil about the ruler of your people."

The future of our nation is not in the hands of our government. God is not looking to the executive, judicial or congressional branches of our government. He has placed the responsibility on one group...us. "If My people..." America's future is completely reliant on our prayer lives. Will we humble ourselves, turn from our wicked ways, pray and seek the face of God? It's up to us.

God, help us to bless our leaders and pray for them! It is easy to criticize. It takes a lot to look beyond the failings and misjudgments, and love the person. We may not approve of everything they do or say, but the love we extend to them, and the prayers in their behalf, will achieve more than any of our rhetoric of intolerance.

In my travels, I have encountered some individuals who are very aggressive in regard to warfare. In an effort to be more strategic, they have bordered on an obsession with demons. People have come to me and informed me of the names of demons who sit as princes over their city. They go on to inform me of the past history of that demon, in which country it originated, and how it was brought to their city. If God has told you to "map" your city, please follow Him, and do not be swayed by my opinion.

I feel, however, that much of this obsession with the names of demons is unfounded. I can find no verse in the Bible to substantiate the need for the name of a demon. What concerns me is that many of the people who "need" to know the name of every demon, don't even know the meanings of all of the names of Jehovah.

There is a man whose ministry has had a tremendous impact on my life and my family. I was going to mention him in the book, but his name slips my mind. Maybe I'll remember it later.

Do you see what an insult it is for me to forget the name of someone who is supposedly important to me? If I walk up to a friend and say, "Hey, what's your name...." I have insulted him. Why would you want to dignify a demon by calling him by his proper name? Actually, I can't even pronounce the names of most of the demons people have told me about.

Jesus said that we should not rejoice because demons are subject to us, but rather, that our name is written in the Lamb's Book of Life. I believe that what He meant was, "Never get more excited over how you relate to demons than your relationship to God." Keep it in perspective.

My suggestion to you is that you spend more time praying in the Spirit than you do in English. In Romans 8:26-27, we are told that God's Spirit makes intercession for us according to God's Will, when we pray. God knows the name, address and telephone number of every demon. I prefer to allow Him to direct the warfare activity as I simply pray in the Spirit according to His Will. I have found that when I pray in tongues for twenty to thirty minutes, there is an urgency, almost a warlike attitude that comes over me. I have talked to many others who have experienced the same thing. I believe that, while praying in the Spirit, God leads us into "perfect" spiritual warfare, according to His Will.

At times people have asked me if I felt that their prayers would be unsuccessful because they had forgotten to use proper order or formula in their warfare prayer time. I informed them that, in my opinion, they are putting more faith in their prayer activity than they are in God's ability to know what is needed. This obsession with formulas can weaken our focus and our faith in our times of prayer. May I suggest that you spend extensive periods of time praying in the Spirit. (If you have not yet received the fullness of the Holy Spirit, with the evidence of speaking in other tongues, please visit our website for more information on this subject.) In my opinion, you would do well to pray at least 30 minutes in tongues at a time. You will see a marked change in your spiritual life as you do this on a regular basis.

Recently after enjoying a lunch with some fellow ministers, one of them said to me, "The main purpose for the existence of a child of God on earth is to do warfare with the devil." Although he was at least twenty years older than me, I felt that I had to speak up and respectfully tell him that I differed with him in opinion. He persisted in his contention, and I in mine.

God did not create us for warfare. He created us for fellowship, praise and worship. To deny that is to ignore the purpose for which we were created. In Ephesians 6 we are told to have our feet shod with the preparation of the gospel of peace, not the gospel of war. We do not do warfare for the sake of warfare. We fight to maintain peace.

Don't lose sight of God's purpose for your life. After reading this book, I am sure you can see that I believe very strongly in the principle and the activity of spiritual warfare. I do not feel, however, that warfare should ever be the central focus of our lives.

God spoke to me recently and said, "The most important thing you will ever build in this life is not a reputation, a bank account or a career. It is a relationship." The most important relationship we will ever build is our relationship with God. We fight satan because he seeks to hinder that relationship.

In John, chapter 12 some Greeks came to worship at the feast. They had heard the stories of Jesus. They wanted to meet Him. They came to Philip and said, in verse 21, "Sir, we would see Jesus."

Concentrate on "seeing Jesus".

Keep your eyes on Jesus, and you won't go wrong.

Sponsors

Ana Antunes
Euclid Antunes
Philip Antunes
Cassandra Antunes
Sarah Antunes
Bruce & BJ Arland
Reverend Daniel Armstrong
Mary Ann Bailly
Kip & Angie Baker
Michael & Jan Baudat
Roger and Martha Beck
Patricia A Bennett
Rev. & Mrs. Garland Bilbo
Lisa Boilore
Mr. & Mrs. Curtis Boudreaux
Margaret Joyce Boudreaux
Daniel & Olivia Bourne
James Brackett
Juergen & Sally Brinner
Rhoda Broome
Dr. & Mrs Willie G. Brown
JJ Brun
Mark & Hiliary Burns
Jerry Caniglia
Doug & Cynthia Canna
Mr. & Mrs. Gene Capdeboscq
Jeremiah Clements
William Clements
David & Barbara Coker

Matt & Beth Cooley
Rod & Lori Coons
Michael & Debbie Cooper
Kathleen Courtois
Curtis & Debi Cradic
Frances M. Daidone
Louie & Leslie DeCamp
John & Diana Delin
Dennis Cooper Delisle
Dennis & Lori Delisle
Dennis & Sharon Delisle
Jayden Nathaniel Delisle
Joseph Reo Delisle
Charles & Mary Frances Denton
Suzanne Dotts
Troy & Tracy Duhon
Rick & Pat Eldred
Hyeran and Bob Eng
Mr. & Mrs. Richard Everett
Pamela J Finney
Scott & Jo Ellen Fischer
Joseph & Brigitte Fleming
Gerald Flottmann DVM
Hans & Debbie Frick
Karen Furuichi
Daniel Giordano, II
Leslie Goodman
Rick & Dianne Goodman
Dr. & Mrs. Marvin E Gorman
Rev Randy & Janice Gorman
James & Kathryn Goss

Doug & Lisa Granger
Len & Beatrix Griffin
David & Susan Grimaldi
Timothy Groves
Jack and Lisa Haines
Rodger Hamel
Juanita Haralson
Tommy & Lesia Harper
TJ Harris
Fred & Linda Harteis
Jerry & Polly Harteis
Don & Janet Held
Jon C Henshaw
Heath and Lindsey Hines
David Alan Hoag
Dan Holcomb, Jr.
Rene' Holcomb
Taylor Holcomb
Whitney Holcomb
Helen Huebner
Barney Huie
Robert & Marie Hurtig
IED Consultancy Pte Ltd.
Alan Isabella
Ana Isabella
Allan Johnson
Christy & Mark Johnson
Apostle John & Helena Kelly
Rhea Kelsall
Louis & Mickey King
Mr. & Mrs. Knorr

Richard & Debra Kluskiewicz
Dick & Anne Laese
Terry and Colene Lange
John & Corine Lawless
Ron Lederle
Kathy Leicester
Merle & Barb Lewis
Edmund Liu
May Liu
Daniel & Lisa Madsen
Dr. Ken Marek
Ronda J Martinez
John & Suzi Mennel and family
Dane & Jackie Meyer
Thomas Meyer
Ross & Brandi McMillan
Geary & Nancy Morrill
Bradley Mitchell
Jonathan Munger
Robert & Melanie Myers Jr
David & Carol Nelson
David Nelson - In Memory of "Tony Renard Baldini"
Shawn & Angela Newton
James Nichols
Tracy & Michelle Norman
Dave Ober
Karen O'Driscoll
Carolita Olilveros
Randy and Kathryn Ollett
Colleen Olson
Judi Olson

Thomas & Christine Ondrea

Marvin R Parazoo

David & Tammy Pianalto

John & Shanna Picinic

Michael Pipes

Frederick & Amy Pope

Damian & Carolyn Repolle'

Erin Restemayer

Jamie Restemayer

Jim & Patricia Restemayer

Annette Romero

Sobner & Marie Anne Saint Dic

Jennifer Schalck

Brent & Anita Schneider

Alan, Diana, and Victoria Schmitt

Glenn & Pam Shoffler

Jeffrey & Debbie Smith

Robert and Rebekah Smith

Kevin & Bree Solomon

Mr. & Mrs. Lawrence & Debra South Jones

Wayne L. Standley Jr.

Gerry & Sandy Stanfield

Amy Steele

Joel Steele

Dave & Lilli Stevens

Elizabeth Stevens

Shawn & Amy Stewart

Daniel & Ruthe St-Pierre

Ronald & Ruth Straw – In Memory of "Pete Castelli"

Tina Sweet

Mr. & Mrs. Stanley Sypniewski

Frank & Marilyn Tenerovich
Amy Teske
Nicholas Teske
Steve & Tiffany Thomasson
Michel Veilleux
Bill & Gladys Watchulonis
Zane Wetzel
Don, Susan and Andrew Wheeler
Chad & Sonja Whitaker
Bill & Karen White
Clay & Kimberly White
Kathleen M. White
Apostle H. Daniel Wilson
David & Sandra Wilson
Min & Evelyn Yanagihashi
Tammy Yost

Becoming A Partner

MINISTRY PARTNER

For a seed of $20 per month, you can receive CD of the Month or become an ePartner and receive an MP3 audio file and an electronic newsletter each month.

STRATEGIC PARTNER

Every year Mark believes God for at least 300 people to sow a $1000 seed into this ministry. Mark will commit to pray daily, for one year, for each of our Strategic Partners for three areas of their lives:

- *Household salvation*
- *Healing and health*
- *Abundance in finances*

In addition to Mark praying for you daily, you will also receive your choice of CD of the Month or MP3 of the Month. Our Strategic Partners who sow on a monthly basis will also receive a Strategic Partner Bible personally signed by Mark and his wife, Gina. If you sow a one-time seed of at least $1,000, you will receive two Strategic Partner Bibles.

As a new partner, you will receive:

- Gumbo for the Soul, a four-disc sampler set of The Best of Mark Gorman
- Mark's book, God's Plan for Prosperity

Each month you will receive:

- A New Teaching
- A Newsletter from Gina updating you on the ministry and the Gorman family

To become a Ministry Partner, visit our online store at **www.markgorman.com** or call toll free **866-663-2043**

Special Offer Bundles

THE PROSPERITY BUNDLE INCLUDES:

- ❧ paperback book of God's Plan for Prosperity
- ❧ electronic book of God's Plan for Prosperity
- ❧ 5 audio CDs of Mark's teaching on prosperity, which inspired the book

RETAIL - $110
YOUR COST - $57

SPECIAL OFFER BUNDLES

THE SPIRITUAL WARFARE BUNDLE INCLUDES:

- ❧ paperback book of The Three Heavens
- ❧ electronic book of The Three Heavens
- ❧ 21 audio CDs of Mark's teaching on spiritual warfare, which inspired the book

RETAIL - $350
YOUR COST - $175   *1/2 price of retail value*